Jesus Christ
According to the Old Testament

By Fr. Marin de Boylesve, S.J.

Translated and Annotated by

E.A. Bucchianeri

Jesus Christ
According to the Old Testament

By Fr. Marin de Boylesve, S.J.

Translated and Annotated by

E.A. Bucchianeri

Batalha Publishers
Fatima, Portugal ©2024

This first English edition has been translated and annotated by E.A. Bucchianeri ©2024 from the Third Edition published by Haton, (Paris, 1875) and Leguicheux-Gallienne, (Le Mans, 1875).

ISBN: 978-989-53726-5-2

TABLE OF CONTENTS

<u>APPENDIX</u>

About the Author

Fr. Marin de Boylesve was born on November 28, 1813 at the Château de la Coltrie in the commune of Saint-Lambert de la Potherie near Angers. He came from a distinguished aristocratic family whose name can be traced back many centuries as seen in Abbé Jean-Baptiste Ladvocat's *Dictionnaire historique portatif* (1755). Fr. Marin descended directly from Eslienne Boyliaue (or Boilyeve), the great statesman and the principal adviser of St. Louis IX, King of France. Other illustrious ancestors included intrepid knights, one in particular also named Marin joined the cause of King Henry IV. After the Battle of Arques, the king called him 'his beloved knight', granted him a heredity knighthood in 1597, then was made Seigneur de la Maurouziere in 1598 thereby granting him the right to add three gold fleur-de-lis to the top of his arms and bear the signs of the Order of St. Michel in his escutcheon. He was also appointed lieutenant-general of Anjou and councillor of state as a reward for his dedication. Another Marin Boylesve appears in the family line, the third to hold the name, and was in service to King Louis XIV as manager of his hôtel. Loyal to the French King and to their Catholic faith, many members of the family were forced to emigrate during the French Revolution, but some members stayed behind in their beloved France. Fr. de Boylesve would recall a favourite family story, of how his grandmother was imprisoned in Angers by the Revolutionaries and managed a daring escape on the road during a prisoner transfer to the local castle. While she pretended to pick up a dropped package, a solider kicked her into the ditch. She took the opportunity to flee to a nearby house. However, when they threatened to imprison those harbouring escaped prisoners, she bravely marched straight in to the Revolutionary Office and gave herself up to ensure the safety of those who sheltered her. The revolutionaries did not dare risk upsetting the populace as her father was the former mayor of Angers before the Revolution and loved by the people. They decided to let her return to her father's house.

Fr. de Boylesve was the last direct descendant of his distinguished line, having followed the call to enter the Company of Jesus, or Jesuits, which also is a remarkable story of a predestined vocation. The Jesuits were persecuted due to fears they were growing in power and wealth. Pressured by the royal courts of Europe, Pope Clement XIV suppressed the Society, forcing members of the order to renounce their vows and go into exile. They were expelled from France in 1764. Fr. de Boylesve's mother, Clémentine de Livonnière, made a solemn promise on the day of her wedding that if God permitted the Jesuits to return to France and she was granted a son, she would offer him to the order and entrust him to it. As mentioned, Fr. Marin was born in 1813, a year before 1814 when Pope Pius VII restored the Society. Tragedy struck when Marin's father died, Marin was only ten months old at the time, but keeping her promise his mother dutifully sent him for his education at the age of ten to the Jesuit Fathers of Montmorillon. The moment he arrived at the school and saw a Jesuit for the first time who happened to be the Superior of the college Fr. Michel

Le Blanc, he heard an inner voice say to him: "Little one, that is what you will be."

Fr. de Boylesve entered the school as a student and was destined never to leave the Jesuits. In 1831 he turned eighteen, a year after the July Revolution of 1830, which saw the rightful king to the French throne Charles X overthrown. His heir, Henry V the 'Miracle Child', was forced into exile at the age of ten, his throne usurped by the man who had been approached to be his regent, Louis-Philippe, Duke of Orléans. The events of the times burned the hearts of the faithful as the historical church of the royal family, Saint-Germain-l'Auxerrois, was profaned. Paris was sacked, and wayside devotional crosses and shrines over large areas of France were destroyed as Catholic legitimist symbols of Charles X, even those which had no royal significance or connection to the king.

Fr. Marin had just completed his schooling when he formally announced his decision to enter the Society, the historic events of the previous year and their aftermath no doubt influencing his decision. Writing to his grandmother he declared: "The course of my studies completed I could not remain without doing anything. God will ask us for an exact account of all the moments He gives us. Full of this thought I ardently wished to serve my country and the Church especially. At a time when both are in such great peril, as a Frenchman and as a Christian, I felt the need to throw myself into the thick of the fray. To take place in the first rows under the banners of religion whose triumph alone can bring glory and happiness back to my homeland, to serve immediately under my first head Jesus Christ, to be one of His companions, seemed to me the most glorious at the same time as most useful for my neighbour. Immense advantages, treasures of happiness and glory, the hundredfold from this life of all that I would give to the Lord, all of these promised in the gospel by Jesus Christ, strongly attracted me to be generous. What more could I do than give myself? (...)"

His family strongly opposed, especially as he was the last direct heir to the Boylesve house, but his mother let him go despite the great sacrifice, no doubt she understood God was accepting her promise to give him to the Jesuits, and not just for his education but now was asking for his whole life, a bitter dreg for her down to the last drop of the cup.

He entered the Novitiate in 1831 at Estavayer in the canton of Fribourg in Switzerland with two other students. As they arrived at their new school, they rang the doorbell at the moment the house clock struck three. The Father who received them remarked: "You are entering at the hour of the Sacred Heart." This introduction to a new school would once again give Fr. de Boylesve a sign regarding the future work he would one day accomplish, although on this occasion he did not know it at the time. He made his first vows at the Maison du Passage on October 10, 1833. He studied philosophy and then in 1835 became a supervisor at the Collège de Mélan, a position he held for one year. He remained in the same college until 1842 where he was in succession professor of grammar, humanities and rhetoric. He thoroughly enjoyed his work with the students, writing in 1837:

"I find this job a lot of fun, despite the hardships that come with it. I have forty students; I love them and I try to spare nothing to make them good Christians, educated Christians capable of one day rendering true service to religion and to the state. It is the sight of such a noble ending that sustains and animates me." In the same letter he continues, regarding his concern for his family, "(...) what the only important thing is, is everyone behaving well and does he remember the motto of the family, RELIGIO, PATRIA? For me who gave up everything, even my name which will be extinguished in my person, I remember it, and God grant that I am consumed and that I use myself in the service of one and of the other."

Although renouncing his aristocratic life he never gave up its noble spirit represented by the family motto, an ardent loyalty to the Catholic faith of his forefathers and his country. In the title pages of his texts he included the family crest of three crosses and motto: RELIGIO, PATRIE − "Faith and Country". Those who knew him and his 'military' style ways said he was just like the loyal intrepid knights of old.

At the end of 1842 he returned to France. He took theology courses at Laval for four years. Instinctively he was drawn to the writings of St. Thomas Aquinas and steered clear of new systems that deviated from the philosophical teachings of the Seraphic Doctor. In 1846 theology training completed, Fr. Boylesve was sent by his superiors to Angers, then in his third year at Notre-Dame d'Ay. In 1848 he was appointed to Brugelette, where he occupied the chair of philosophy. One student who fondly recalled Fr. de Boylesve and his time at Brugelette said his arrival was providential. His classes were easy to follow his manner clear and crisp, but this is not all that gained the respect of the students. In 1848 they were restless as revolution was in the air, Louis-Philippe I, who had overthrown Catholic King Charles X was now in his own turn overthrown. Rising above and beyond what was required of his philosophy courses, Fr. Boylesve seized the opportunity like a knight-commander of old to direct the lazy students yet bursting with energy towards something constructive: Catholic action to fashion them into vigorous young men of service for Church and country. With his apostolic action he captivated the students with his literature classes, speaking on many subjects from philosophy, history, politics both ancient and modern. He particularly drew them with his catechism lessons on the Council of Trent, his clarity and enthusiasm captivating them.

As Fr. de Boylesve loved his students he was equally admired and loved by them, earning the nickname 'The Captain' as a mark of respect. The students composed a military style tune for his birthday, the refrain remaining popular and hummed everywhere: "Courageous Captain, lead us into battle." A student recalls: "I understood all that was apostolic about his action on us. We can sum it up by saying that he made it his mission to preach to us always and everywhere the contemplation of Saint Ignatius on the Reign of Jesus Christ as it is given in the Exercises." In 1851 Fr. Boylesve was sent to Vannes where he was made prefect of studies, his nickname 'The Captain' following him. In October 1853 he left the post and resumed teaching philosophy, a position that he would keep for a long time, either in Poitiers or in Vaugirard.

Known to be quiet and reserved when on his own, it was another matter when he was teaching or publicly speaking. He was incapable of remaining silent or softening his direct manner of expression when it was a question of truth, and did not hold back when it came to defend the Faith and the Church against unbelievers, becoming as noted like his knight-ancestor of old, charging forth to give chase and defeat any bold rascal on the field of battle albeit with his tongue and writings rather than with a literal sword.

His attitude is quaintly summed up by the art critique he once gave of the statue of the fountain of St. Michael in Paris, complaining with slight annoyance that the mighty archangel was made to look too carefree and benevolent when dispatching Satan: "See then, it is that he seems to spare him!" He was also a zealous worker and relished activity. He once wrote: "I challenge my superiors to give me too much work."

In addition to his religious duties and teaching, he was a prolific writer, his output seeming to have no end. He wrote on a myriad of subjects and in different genres, from devotional booklets and pamphlets to history, literature, philosophy, Biblical dramas, summaries of the Church Fathers and Doctors, his own sermons, studies of the Scriptures, Our Lady, the Exercises of St. Ignatius just to name a few, there were always more plans for further works in progress, his room filled with notes and notebooks. He was always studying as well, also making it a practise to read through the entire Bible every year. One might call him a workaholic in today's terms, but it was noted he believed in a time and a place for everything and diligently managed his hours. He enjoyed recreation time, especially going for walks, and did not sacrifice rest. Despite his zest for work, he disapproved of a few young professors who sacrificed too much sleep and recreation time for their studies, endangering their health. Yet, while sparing of his time, he was ever charitable and ready to help another all for the glory of God.

In September 1870 Fr. de Boylesve was sent to the College of Le Mans, Notre-Dame de Sainte-Croix, when the Franco-Prussian war was raging and France suffered the indignity of invasion. The humiliation felt by the country also struck the pious and patriotic Fr. de

Boylesve to the core: "I searched through the memories of my life; I do not remember ever having felt greater pain than this, not even when I learned of my mother's death. This humiliation of France, the eldest daughter of the Church, thus succumbing before Prussia, the eldest daughter of Protestantism, in the face of the whole world, is something unheard of."

The Messenger, the magazine of the Apostleship of Prayer run by the Jesuits, began spreading the visions of St. Margaret Mary, declaring the only way France would be saved from her enemies was to embrace the devotion to the Sacred Heart. The message inspired Fr. de Boylesve. He became a chaplain to the Catholic Papal Zouaves, forces sent to defend the French Motherland from the Protestant invaders, giving them rousing sermons: "Clotilde, inspiring faith in Clovis, saved the Franks and slaughtered the Germans at their feet ... Joan of Arc by her standard delivered France from the English! Your standard is the Sacred Heart." The Zouaves placed the Sacred Heart on their banner. Fr. de Boylesve also busily spread Sacred Heart badges of wool for the soldiers to pin on their uniforms, for they were in high demand. A gifted and inspiring preacher, his sermons encouraged them onward, even when they were driven back in defeat by the Prussians to where the soldiers remarked: "This man can lead us to the fire tomorrow; we would gladly be killed for him."

Fr. de Boylesve is fondly remembered today in Catholic circles in France for his work as the director of the Apostleship of Prayer in Le Mans through which he contributed to the spread of devotion to the Sacred Heart. On October 17, 1870 Fr de Boylesve was appointed to preach at the Visitation of Le Mans upon St. Margaret Mary for his subject, who at the time was a Blessed. He also preached upon another mystic who had died within their own times, Mother Marie de Jesus (1797-1854) from the convent des Oiseaux of Paris who had received revelations from the Sacred Heart that were favourably recognised by the Archbishop of Paris. On June 21, 1823 the Sacred Heart revealed to Sr. Marie that He desired France be consecrated to His Sacred Heart by the King, and that a chapel be built and dedicated to Him, and the feast of the national consecration be formally celebrated every year. "After my sermon," recounts Fr. Boylesve, "the Mother Superior expressed to me her astonishment at my silence with regard to an almost similar order that Our Lord had given to Blessed Margaret Mary on June 17th, 1689. I confessed that in our college, which had barely opened for a month, I had not found the letters of the Blessed One and that I was unaware of the apparition and the order she was telling me about. I promised to make good this omission." Apparently at that time, the Sacred Heart's requests to St. Margaret Mary for a shrine and the national consecration of France by the King were not yet widely known.

True to his word, filled with his characteristic zeal for faith and country, doing what he could to extend the reign of Jesus Christ through his beloved homeland and secure its safety, the very next day he repaired his omission by publishing a pamphlet featuring the prophecies of St. Margaret Mary and Mother Marie de Jesus entitled "Triumph of France by the Sacred Heart", composing a special prayer of consecration to be said, which the Zouaves said every Friday as hope in the Sacred Heart was sorely needed.

Paris was threatened with destruction by bombardments, then starvation by the invading Prussians, having commenced a siege around the city in September 1870. The siege continued until January 1871, the citizens reduced to dire circumstances. The zoo animals were slaughtered for food, the populace also living off of stray animals and rats. While the Prussian advance had ceased, humiliation still ensued when France suffered defeat at the hands of the Prussians with the establishment of the German Empire, also losing the territory of the Alsace-Lorraine to the victors. The troubles were not over. From March to May 1871 Paris fell into the clutches of the anticlerical socialist Communards, rebels revolting against the new government of the Third Republic. Blood ran in the streets, historical buildings burned, including the Tuileries Palace. The anticlerical Communards also executed the Archbishop of Paris, Georges Darboy, fulfilling the prophecy of St. Catherine Laboure. This horrific turn of events, combined with the circulation of prophecies foretelling the destruction of Paris was at hand, the faithful no doubt felt doom hung over the city. The times were desperate. After several reprintings, including a full reproduction of the text by Fr. Ramiere in the 'Messenger' newsletter issued by the Apostleship of Prayer, more than 330,000 copies of Fr. de Boylesve's pamphlets of the 'Triumph of the Sacred Heart' were circulated. It contributed to the rapid spread devotion to the Sacred Heart and bolstered the call to have the Universal Church consecrated to the Sacred Heart, also to build a national shrine on Montmartre in atonement for the atrocities committed by the Communards who began their uprising there. Construction began in 1875, the cornerstone was laid on June 16, 1875, the day Bl. Pius IX encouraged all the faithful to pray the consecration to the Sacred Heart using the special formula composed by the Sacred Congregation of Rites for the 200th anniversary of the apparition of the Sacred Heart to St. Margaret Mary. The construction of Sacre Coeur was at last completed in 1914.

As for Fr. Boylesve, in addition to his efforts to spread devotion to the Sacred Heart he worked unceasingly at many other endeavours, not only as director of the Apostolate of Prayer in Le Mans, but also with the Confraternities of Saint Joseph such as that of the Good Death, and also the Confraternity of the Agonizing Heart, the Work of Campaigns, Conferences of St. Vincent de Paul, Workers' Circles, he still appeared to dare all and sundry that they would never be able to find enough work for him to do. He amazed all that he was never at a loss for a subject to preach upon. He could easily vary his sermons to where it appeared he never preached the same way twice, and always captured his hearers' attention. One day out of curiosity a hardened sinner walked in to listen to him preach and left a converted man.

He also continued his prolific writing, it is evident his gift for giving interesting and encouraging sermons had transferred to his pages, which this book is also proof. His explanations of the Scriptures and Christ's Kingship are crisp, clear, and easy to comprehend. His texts remain just as inspiring today as when they were penned well over a century ago.

When Fr. Boylesve wasn't working, he was praying. There was no question that he maintained a deep spiritual life. He was transferred to Vaugirard in 1875, returning to Le Mans two years later in 1877. Three years later his teaching came to an end at the college there with the decree of March 29, 1880 issued by the French minister for public education prohibiting the Jesuits from engaging in their educational apostolate, only the first of several anticlerical laws that would be passed in France over the next decades. Fr. Boylesve admitted he was on the verge of tears saying his last Mass for the students in the chapel before the school closed. Yet, he remained as active as ever despite this terrible blow, preaching, giving catechisms and continuing his writing, tackling the problems of their day threatening both the Church and society.

He continued working despite his old age, until the end of 1891 when his activity was curtailed. He was struck with various ailments, first a tormenting dermatitis that remained with him, then inflammation of the blood that restricted his activities for many weeks, although he managed to say Mass and continue his writing, until at last he was struck with paralysis, unable to walk or speak. Clutching his rosary and his crucifix, the ever zealous 'priest-knight' of the Vendée gave up his soul to God in February 22, 1892 and was buried in the Jesuit cemetery of Sainte-Croix.[1]

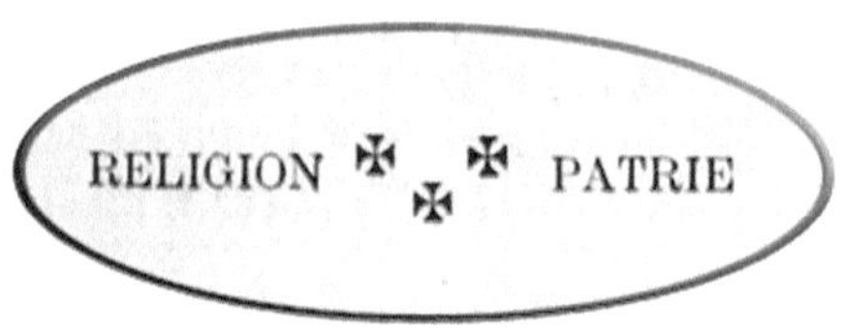

---

1   Biographical information from 'Necrologie. Le Père Marin de Boylesve', in 'Lettres de Jersey', Vol. XII, No. 1 (April 1893)

About this Edition

This first ever English translation was made from the Third edition published by Haton, (Paris, 1875) and Leguicheux-Gallienne, (Le Mans, 1875) British spelling has been used. New material includes a biography of the author, footnotes, the appendix, and the illustrations.

E.A. Bucchianeri

The Reign of Christ

Jesus is the Christ, the Anointed One, that is to say, the King yesterday and today, and, He will be so tomorrow and after. *'Jesus Christus, heri et hodie: ipse in saecula.'* "Jesus Christ, yesterday, and today; and the same for ever." - (Hebrews 13:8). Therefore it needs be He must reign: *'Oportet illum regnare,'* "For He must reign - (until He hath put all his enemies under His feet.)" (1 Cor. 15:25). He must reign until He has reduced all of His enemies to serve as His footstool. [2]

Woe to that nation, woe to that king who refuses to submit to Him. If Jesus must reign, by the same token it is necessary that every kingdom contrary to His kingdom must perish: *'Gens enim et regnum quod non servierit tibi peribit.'* - "For the nation and the kingdom that will not serve thee, shall perish," - (Isaiah 60:12)

Let us go back beyond time and seek within God Himself the reason for this necessary Kingship of Jesus.

---

2 A reference to the prophecy of David in Psalm 109: (1-2): "The Lord said to my Lord: Sit thou at my right hand: Until I make thy enemies thy footstool. The Lord will send forth the sceptre of thy power out of Sion: rule thou in the midst of thy enemies."

God

God was alone: alone in His Eternity, alone in His Immensity. Outside of Him — there is *nothing* — nothing but nothingness and silence. *'Ipse enim solus est.'* ("For He is alone," Job 23: 13)

God Is, and He knows it, and He also says it to Himself: "I Am Who Am." - *'Ego sum qui sum.'* (Exodus 3:14)

God knows Himself, God asserts Himself, and knowing Himself and asserting Himself, He generates His word, His *Word*, His Image, His only Son, wisdom of His Intelligence, splendour of His Glory. From all eternity God is Father, because He is never without knowing Himself and affirming Himself in Himself. From all eternity the Son is God, otherwise there would be an instant where God would be without knowing Himself, without asserting Himself, without being the *Father*.[3] "In the beginning was the Word, and the Word was with God, and the Word was God" : *'In principio erat Verbum, et Verbum erat apud Deum, et Deus erat Verbum.'* (John 1:1)

"You are My Son," said the Lord to His Word, "today, in the day of My Eternity, in this day that never begins and never ends, in this moment that always was and always will be, today I have begotten You" - *'Dominus dixit ad me: Filius meus es tu, ego hodie*

---

[3]   God cannot lie, nor speak an untruth, nor can He be without knowledge of Himself. As He declared He had 'begotten' a Son, then the Son of God exists, and the Son is also God.

genui te.' - ("The Lord hath said to me: Thou art my son, this day have I begotten thee," - Psalm 2:7)

Before Lucifer, before the light, when nothing yet existed but Me, I begot You, '*Ex utero ante Luciferum genui te.*' ("... from the womb before the day star I begot thee," Psalm 109:3)

I gave You My Being, I gave You My Essence, I gave You My Nature, I gave You My Substance, I gave You My Intelligence, I gave You My Power. You resemble Me, and not only do You resemble Me, but You are My equal; like Me, Eternal, Immense, Infinite in Your Being, Infinite in Intelligence, Infinite in Power, You are My Son; '*Filius meus es tu.*' ("Thou art My Son, this day have I begotten Thee," Psalm 2:7)

The Father and the Son love each other with an eternal love. From this mutual Love proceeds the Divine Breath, 'spiritus', the Holy Spirit, eternal bond of the Father and the Son.

To the Father, principle of the Son and, with the Son, principle of the Holy Spirit: is Power. To the Son, Word of the Father: is Wisdom. To the Holy Spirit, Love of both the Father and the Son: is Goodness.

But, the Son and the Holy Spirit are Almighty with the Almighty Power of the Father. The Wisdom of the Son is the Wisdom of the Father and the Holy Spirit. The Father and the Son are infinitely Good from the very Goodness that They give to the Holy Spirit.

God is therefore alone; for there is only one God: '*Ego sum solus et praeter me non est alius*', "I alone Am, and there is no other God than Me." (Deut. 32:39) And yet, in what seems like a contradiction, in His immense solitude, in His eternal silence, God is *not* alone because in His unity Three Persons subsist, the Father, the Son and the Holy Spirit. Therefore God is indeed 'alone', that is, by the unity of His Being as One: '*natura unus*': yet He is *not* alone, because of the Trinity of Persons: '*personis trinus – trinus et unus*'.

The Father is God, the Son is God, the Holy Spirit is God. And these are not three gods, but Three Persons in One God.

The Father is not the Son, and the Son is not the Father, for the Father *begets* the Son and the Son is *begotten* by the Father. To beget and to be begotten are opposite relationships.

The Holy Spirit is not the Father nor the Son. The Father and the Son are not the Holy Spirit. For the Holy Spirit proceeds from the Father and the Son by a common breath, producing the Holy Spirit. Producing and being produced are opposite relationships.

In Their Eternity the Father, the Son and the Holy Spirit enjoy a glory and beatitude that is immense, immutable, infinite. What could be lacking in Him Who, by Himself and in Himself, Is and possesses the Sovereign Good? What could be missing for the One Who in His perfect unity, in His absolute simplicity, finds an inseparable society in Three Persons Who are One God?

God could therefore remain alone. But out of pure goodness, He wanted to associate His Goodness with beings capable of enjoying it. Infinitely wise, He wanted to create beings capable of knowing. Infinitely good, He wanted to create beings capable of loving. He drew forth intelligent and free beings, not from Himself, for He is One, simple and indivisible, but instead, drew them from nothing. He willed, and He made what was once not, to be and to exist. He willed it, and it is done. *'Quaecumque voluit, fecit.'* ("But our God is in heaven: he hath done all things whatsoever he would," Psalm 113:11)

He simply said: it is done: *'Dixit et facta sunt'* - "For He spoke and they were made", ("For he spoke and they were made, he commanded and they were created," - Psalm 32:9)

The Angels

Apart from God, there exited *nothing*. God wills, God speaks. Suddenly, millions of pure spirits tremble around the majesty of the Thrice Holy God.

Happy to exist, happy to know, happy to will, the angel knows himself and he loves himself: he is so beautiful, he is so good! But at the same moment, withdrawing into himself, he recognizes that just a little moment earlier, *he was not there.* Where is he from? *Where* does he come from? Who has done this? Immediately, at the same time as he knows and loves himself, and by the same act which makes him know and love himself, he recognizes the One Who alone is by Himself and through Whom alone he could come to be. Recognizing the supreme majesty of Him Who Is, he adores Him with happiness; recognizing the sovereign goodness of Him Who made him what he is, he loves Him with inexpressible joy. Adoration of the Most High God, such is the first impulse, the first act of angelic intelligence. Love of the Most Good God, such is the first movement, the first act of the will of these noble and free spirits.

But who can speak of the marvellous order of the host of angels? Ranked according to the varying degrees of their natural perfection, functions and duties, they are divided into three hierarchies, each of which contains three choirs.

At the lowest rank come the *Angels*, who one day will be in charge of guarding men; then come the *Archangels* who will watch over the superiors of human communities; the *Principalities* are next, who will direct the various societies formed between men. These three choirs make up the first hierarchy.

To the second hierarchy belongs the *Powers*, whose mission is to preside over the order of the material world; next, the *Virtues*, which God will use to bring about those effects superior to the laws of nature which we call miracles ; then, the *Dominations*, who like the generals of our armies, are responsible for presiding over the execution of the orders of the Most High.

In the third and highest hierarchy first come the *Thrones*, through which God communicates His orders for the government of the two worlds, the material world and the spiritual world; then, next highest in rank, the *Cherubim*, who all illuminated with the splendours of Divine Intelligence, reflect Its clarity on all celestial intelligences; finally, the highest of all the angelic choirs, the *Seraphim*, who all ablaze with the ardour of Divine Love, spread Its fiery rays over all the angelic wills.

In the centre of this great host sparkling with light and fire, the angel whom God had established as the supreme head of all the choirs and of all the celestial hierarchies shone with incomparable brilliance. His name was Lucifer, or 'The Illuminator'.[4] To see him as Ezekiel describes him, he looks like a sun rolling in the middle of a dazzling multitude of burning diamonds, all the rays of which it reflects at the same time while it itself illuminates them with all its lights.[5] But, however brilliant they may be, let us leave the pictorial images, they will always fall short of reality.

---

4 Also, 'Light-bearer'.

5 Fr de Boylesve must have had in mind the prophetic passage in Ezekiel that refers to the King of Tyre and his downfall, which also doubles as a description of a cherub in Paradise that was perfect and surrounded by shining stones of fire until he fell. *"Thou wast in the pleasures of the paradise of God: every precious stone was thy covering: (...) Thou a cherub stretched out, and protecting, and I set thee in the holy mountain of God, thou hast walked in the midst of the stones of fire. Thou wast perfect in thy ways from the day of thy creation, until iniquity was found in thee. (...) and I cast thee out from the mountain of God, and destroyed thee, O covering cherub, out of the midst of the stones of fire."* (Ezekiel 28: 13-16) Considering this refers to a great fallen angel of the highest hierarchy, Lucifer must have been meant, even if Lucifer was a seraph and not a cherub since Lucifer is also described as being cast out from attempting to place himself above the stars and on the mountain of God by Isaiah (14:12-13): *"How art thou fallen from heaven, O Lucifer, who didst rise in the morning? How art thou fallen to the earth, that didst wound the nations. And thou saidst in thy heart: I will ascend into heaven, I will exalt my throne above the stars of God, I will sit in the mountain of the covenant, in the sides of the north."*

The World

Next, God will bring forth His Wisdom, His Goodness, His Power through wonders of another nature. At the Voice of the Most High nothingness became chaos.[6] Was it not at first a confused, shapeless, inert mass, a frightful jumble of all the atoms? At this sight, the astonished angels all cried out at once: "The Lord is great, His greatness has no end." - *'Magnus Dominus et non habet finem.'* ("The Lord is great ... and hath no end.")[7]

Chaos will become the world. Out of this confusion comes order; and by condensing on the order of the Word and under the impulse of the creative Spirit, the atoms will become the suns and the earths.[8]

---

6   'Chaos' – When God made heaven and earth, "... the earth was void and empty, and darkness was upon the face of the deep," (Genesis, 1:2). There was no order yet placed on these very first elements of created matter, and so, there was 'chaos': which is defined as *'a state of utter confusion or disorder; a total lack of organization or order'.*

7   Apparently, a shortened combination of this verse from Baruch (3:25) *"Magnus est, et non habet finem"*, 'It is great and hath no end', and Psalm 134 (v. 5): *"Quia ego cognovi quod magnus est Dominus, et Deus noster prae omnibus diis."* - 'For I have known that the Lord is great, and our God is above all gods'.

8   A reference to the creation of the outer cosmos of the heavens with its stars and planets.

God creates light over the waters

Six times the Word of the All Powerful will burst into space; six days will respond to the Voice of the Supreme Ordinator.

God said: "Let there be light," - '*Fiat Lux*' – and the light shone.
And the delighted angels cried out at once: "The Lord is great, His greatness has no end." - '*Magnus Dominus et non habet finem.*'

God speaks again; the sky strengthens and expands; the earth rises from the middle of the waters and is covered with plants which have within them the principle of life; the suns roll in their light and mark the times;[9] the waters are populated with fish, and birds soar into the air; the most varied animals move upon the face of the earth.

Ever more delighted, the angels never tire of saying: "The Lord is great, His greatness has no end." - *'Magnus Dominus et non habet finem.'*

---

9   A reference to the sun, and the stars as they are also suns and mark signs and seasons.   The French can also poetically refer to the light coming from the sun as 'soleil', so the moon could also be referred to here as well as its light comes from the sun.

<u>Man</u>

The temporal palace so to speak is prepared, it awaits its king.   The temporal temple is completed it awaits its pontiff.   God brought forth from out of nothing two natures which seem like two opposite poles set apart from each other: spirit and matter. Who can measure the distance from the simple atom to the foremost of the seraphim? Already without doubt, under the influence of the creative Word, the scale of beings has risen from degree to degree: from simple matter, next to inert substance, then to movement received and preserved; from external movement to this intimate movement which is called life, then, from life to sense and instinct.   But from the most gifted animal on earth to the lowest pure spirit of heaven, still, what a distance!   Here God stops, He collects Himself, He takes counsel, He speaks to Himself and thus speaking to Himself alone, He nevertheless speaks to several. Let us listen; it is the first indication of the Divine Trinity to be found in the holy books.

One of the Three Persons speaking to the Others, or, all Three speaking together, God said: "Let us make man to our image and likeness." - *'Faciamus hominem ad imaginem et similitudinem nostram'*. (Gen. 1:26)

With that said, the All Powerful combines together in a little mud all the material elements: the earth, water, air and fire. From all this the Divine Worker fashions a body, thereby summarizing all the wonders of the six days. All that is missing from this masterpiece is life.

The Angels admired, they waited, when suddenly the Divine Breath communicated to this marvellous body the gift of life, senses, and something more. If we are allowed to imagine what then happened, I seem to see this new creature rising up by himself by the virtue of that interior principle of force and life that the Divine Breath communicated to him. I see him raising his hands and eyes to heaven. The expression of his gaze and the sound of his voice announce that there is a new intelligence in the world and that the union has been made between matter and spirit. This marvellous being, in whom God united all that He created, is Man.

The God-Man

God has finished His work. He returns to His eternal rest. Man and Angel are called to take part in it. But, they must have the glory of meriting this happiness.

What the Angels' test was, and at what moment it was proposed to them, we do not know. Whether on the first day, or later, as the fall of the rebel angel thrown from heaven into the earth seems to insinuate: - "I have cast thee to the ground," - '*In terram projeci te*', (Ezekiel 28:17), by bringing together the various traits of the Scriptures, we can suppose that these things happened[10] in approximately the following order:

Hidden in the splendours of His glory, but still visible through His works,[11] God thus reveals Himself to the Angels, and speaking to them in the way that spirits speak, He affirms Himself, He names Himself: I Am Who Am - '*ego sum qui sum*'. And the Angels all in one voice cried out: "Come, let us worship Him." - '*Venite, adoremus.*' (Psalm 94:6)

The Divine Voice continued: Three bear witness in heaven, the Father, the Word, the Holy Spirit: and these Three are One. '*Quoniam tres sunt qui testimonium dant in caelo, Pater, Verbum et Spiritus Sanctus: et hi tres unum sunt.*' (1 John 5:7) This is the express revelation of the Trinity of Persons in the unity of the Divine Being; it is the implicit announcement of the One to Whom Three bear witness in heaven. Who is it? A little moment longer then the angels will know.

---

10   That is, Fr de Boylesve is saying the Scriptures do not literally state outright what the great test of the Angels was before they could be admitted to Heaven, nor precisely when they were tested. However, we can deduce certain details from the Scriptures as he notes the passage in Ezekiel describing Lucifer's fall indicates it must have occurred sometime when God began creating the physical earth as Lucifer is cast to the *ground* in punishment. Fr de Boylesve then notes it is possible to glean other details regarding their test and put events into an approximate order of occurrence.

11   As part of the test, God did not reveal the Beatific vision yet to the Angels, they were placed in an outer part of Heaven called they Empyrean heaven and did not see God in His full glory. However, if they witnessed the creation of the cosmos and the earth as Ezekiel suggests, then they indeed were able to know God through His works and what He did reveal to them as the Creator. His greatness was made manifest despite hiding the full greatness of His glory.

However, as soon as the mystery of the Trinity was revealed to them, covering their faces with their wings, they said to one another: "Holy, holy, holy is the Lord, the God of hosts; the whole earth is full of His glory." - *'Sanctus, sanctus, sanctus Dominus Deus exercituum; plen est omnis terra gloria ejus'.* (Isaiah 6:3)

God will now initiate them into the grand secret of His plan. He first created pure spirits, He then created material beings, then, He united spirit and matter in Man. It is still not enough. In His wisdom and goodness He intends something even more wonderful, and His power is great enough to accomplish the design He has conceived.

A day will come when the Second Person of the August Trinity, the Word, uniting with a creature, will elevate this creature so high by this union that, without losing the nature which is proper to it, this privileged being will nevertheless be but one and the same person with the Word.

Who will be the creature called to this sublimity? Will it be the Angel? Or Mankind? It will not be the Angel. It will be Man, who although inferior to the Angel by his nature, has over him the advantage of summarizing in his body and in his soul all the genres and all the degrees of creation.

God will became a Man. The Word will become flesh: "Adore Him, O you who are his angels." *'Adorate eum, omnes angeli ejus.'* - (Psalm 96:7 – Hebrews 1:6)

There was then a solemn silence in heaven. The new mystery so exceeded their expectations that the most sublime seraphim could only hide their faces.

<u>Lucifer</u>

There was an angel who shone above all the others with the brilliance of his genius. God was pleased to adorn him with all His gifts and He made him like the sun among the angelic spheres. His name clearly indicates what his glory and mission were. His name was Lucifer, the 'light bearer', the 'illuminator'. Leader of the celestial militias, it was up to him to make the first declaration of fidelity among the angels; to him fell the honour to be the first to adore in advance the Word made flesh, it was granted to him to be the first to swear faith and homage to the future King of all of creation. The angels were waiting for him to speak, and Lucifer spoke.

I will ascend to heaven, but I will ascend by myself, by the sole force of my intelligence, and not by the submission of faith; I will ascend by the sole virtue of my power, and not by the help of grace. - *'In coelum conscendam'* - "*I* will ascend to Heaven," (Isaiah 14:12-13; "How art thou fallen from heaven, O Lucifer, who didst rise in the morning? ... Thou saidst in thy heart: *I will ascend into heaven.*")

'I will exalt my throne above the stars of God.' - *'Super star Dei exaltabo solium meum'.* (Isaiah 14:13) These stars were neither the physical stars nor the suns.[12] By their very nature, the least of the angels are above the most sparkling star. Lucifer, in his supreme disdain, claims to establish himself *by his own strength* above all the angels, mainly, above those who

---

12 That is, the other suns in the cosmos.

through their fidelity will especially become the angels of God.

'I will sit on the mountain of the Testament.' - *'Sedebo in monte Testamenti'*. (Isaiah 14: 13)[13] In scriptural language the Testament is the covenant between God and His creature, in particular, between God and man. The 'mountain' of the Testament is the culmination, the highest degree of alliance, of the union between God and the created being. When

---

13 The Douay-Rheims version: "I will sit in the mountain of the covenant."

Lucifer then exclaims: 'I will sit on the mountain of the Testament,' it is as if he had said: 'God wants to unite Himself to man and thereby elevate him to the highest possible degree of creation; I will climb higher still and thereby sit above the Word made flesh: *'Sedebo in monte Testamenti'*.

Lucifer continues: In vain this great God hides in the depths of His infinity, I will penetrate into the bosom of the night in which He envelops Himself and in which He hides from the gaze of the highest intelligences,[14] and I penetrate into 'the sides of the north': - *'In lateribus aquilonis'*. (Isaiah 14:13)

From there 'I will ascend above the height of the clouds.' - *'Ascendam super altitudinem nubium.'* (Isaiah 14:14)

Piercing solely by my intelligence the cloud which veils the mystery of the Divine Essence from every created spirit, that is to say, the Trinity of Persons in one God, I will *by myself* unite myself to the Divine Word, and, seeing God as He sees Himself, 'I will be like the Most High,' - *'Similis ero Altissimo'*. (Isaiah 14:14)

Lucifer has spoken. Astonishment, no doubt, must have been at its height among the celestial phalanxes: a tribute was awaited, but it was revolt that raised its red standard. Soon, a dull murmur runs through the angelic ranks, it rumbles, it grows, it rises and suddenly gains formidable proportions, it bursts

---

14   Fr de Boylesve is referring to God keeping the Beatific Vision hidden from them at that point, as they were placed in the Empyrean Heaven and not in the highest Heavens until they passed the test. Lucifer, in his pride, boasts he will attempt to rise up to Heaven into the Beatific Vision himself by his own power.

like lightning and rolls like thunder. Thousands of voices join with Lucifer: 'I will ascend,' - '*ascendam*'; I will be like the Most High, '*similis ero Altissimo*'. This God-made-Man Whom I must adore now in advance and Whom one day I will have to serve, no, I will not serve Him: '*Non serviam*'. ("I will not serve," Jeremiah 2:20). It was like the waves of a storm rushing from all sides at once in order to carry these threats of pride to the Most High. And that is what the voice of one individual can do!

<u>Michael</u>

But suddenly in the middle of this immense clamour three words resounded: three words brief and sharp like lightning that criss-crosses through the clouds, three words which, terrible as lightning, burst upon the rebel phalanxes like three claps of thunder:

MI-CHA-EL – '*quis ut Deus*' – who is like unto God?

He was also alone, the noble archangel when he dared to cast this simple but bold protest before the triumphing Lucifer. 'In your mad pride, you cried out: - I will be like the Most High - '*similis ero Altissimo*'. Already around you a third of the angels repeat: '*Similis ero Altissimo*', I will be like the Most High. -- *But who is like God, 'quis ut Deus'?*'

In Hebrew MI-CHA-EL.

A noble and valiant challenge, a generous war cry, which will become the name of the intrepid archangel.

One voice was enough to lead millions of intelligences into the revolts of pride, and, one was enough to rally the immense majority of celestial spirits to the flag of loyalty.

Never say, 'I am alone.' Do not be alarmed by the number of the enemies against God, nor by the multitude of the crowd and the boasting of their words. Even if you were alone, declare yourself. The good ones are just waiting for a leader to rise and a signal to be sent. Three words will be enough to disconcert pride and put down the insolence of their speeches.

Meanwhile, "there was a great battle in heaven, Michael and his angels fought with the dragon, and the dragon fought and his angels" - *'Et factum est praelium magnum in caelo : Michael et angeli ejus praeliabantur cum dracone, et draco pugnabat, et angeli ejus,'* (Apocalypse 12:7)

When faced with the truth, sophism remains mute, but more often than not, it persists in falsehood.

In the presence of the Archangel Michael's firm but striking question, Lucifer did not respond, but, he did not surrender either. Finally, after giving the faithful angels time to cover themselves with glory through the heroism of resistance, God will crown their valour with a brilliant victory. Suddenly, from the very bosom of Lucifer, to use the energetic language of the prophet, comes forth a devouring fire which, without consuming him, reduces all his efforts and all his power to nothing. "Therefore I will bring forth a fire from the midst of thee, to devour thee ... thou art brought to nothing, and thou shalt never be any more." - *'Producam ergo ignem de medio tui, qui comedat te. ... Nihili factus es et non eris in perpetuum.'* (Ezekiel 28:18-19)

The angel who just now had burst forth so brilliantly and proudly, falls from the summit of creation in the blink of an eye, dragging with him a third of the stars, that is to say, a third of the celestial spirits that had become accomplices of his pride. Precipitated from the heights of the heavens, perhaps from the centre of all the sidereal spheres, and launched into space, they tumble in a frightful

disorder and fall from abyss to abyss only to finally stop at the extremity of the world, in that fiery underground, in that eternal night which is called hell. "I cast thee out from the mountain of God ... I have cast thee to the ground." - '*Et ejeci te de monte Dei... in terram projeci te.*' - (Ezekiel 28:16-17, Apoc. 12:9)

Thus ended the first combat. The pride of the rebels remains powerless, and their place is no longer found in heaven. "And they prevailed not, neither was their place found any more in heaven " - '*Et non valuerunt, neque locus inventus est eorum amplius in caelo.*' (Apoc. 12:8)

Such was the outcome of the first revolution.

The Serpent

"Woe to the earth, woe to the sea: (for Lucifer, having become) the devil, has come down in great wrath, knowing that he has little time." (Apoc. 12:12) Seeing himself thrown to the earth, the dragon began to pursue the Woman; he declared war on all the children of the Woman who bear the testimony of Jesus Christ, (Apoc. 12:17) - "and he stood on the sand that borders the sea,"- '*et stetit supra arenam maris.*' (Apoc. 12:18)

The sea, in the language of the Bible, represents the nations, which in fact, follow each other one after another like the waves of the ocean. Satan has sworn eternal hatred to the Woman, because she must be the Mother of this God-Man Whom he refused to worship.

First in the form of the serpent he pursued Eve, future mother of the human race; then Mary, Mother of the God-Man; then, he pursues the Church, Mother of those who bear the testimony of Jesus Christ. What vain fury! Proud and great as he is, Satan rests only on sand, and on the sand of the sea, that is, on the shifting sand of revolutions: '*stetit supra arenam maris*'. Let us look back for a moment and study the origins.

God said to the man and the woman; Increase, multiply, populate the earth and subdue it. He had placed them in a delightful paradise; and to provide them with a means of showing their loyalty and deserving even greater happiness, He said to them: "You may eat of all the fruits of this garden, except that of the tree of the knowledge of good and evil. The day you eat it, you will die." (Gen. 2:16-17) Presented with such an easy condition, Adam and Eve must have believed their future was assured.

But here comes Satan. Disguised in the form of a serpent, he spies on the moment when the woman finds herself alone, and addressing her as the weakest: "Why," he said to her, "why has God commanded you not to eat of all the fruits of this garden?" (Gen. 3:1)

"Why?" This is the first word of revolution, which, since the beginning of time, has been summed up in this formula: "Why should it be for *me* to obey, while *that* one gets to command?"

"Why?" A difficult question when it is addressed to anyone other than God, when the one who must answer cannot easily demonstrate that it is in the name of God that he speaks and commands. But when the question is *addressed to God Himself*, it becomes as senseless as it is insolent, and the answer is easily plain.

Why? God is Wisdom, Goodness, Power itself. Sovereignly wise, He orders nothing without good reason; He knows *exactly* what is best for me and what is not. Infinitely good, *He cannot let anything happen against me unless it is for my good.* Almighty, He will know how to make Himself obeyed, or punish disobedience. For every difficulty regarding the question "why", as for every murmur, this answer suffices.

Eve knew this. But she had the imprudence or the curiosity to listen to the serpent to the end; then, she had the imprudence or the vanity to respond. Upon hearing the serpent, one would have said that *all* the fruits of the garden were forbidden: "Why has God commanded you not to eat of *all* the fruits of this garden?" "We can," replies the woman, "we can eat from all the fruits, except those from the tree in the middle of the garden; God has commanded us not to eat it." The answer so far is wise and true, but Eve *adds to her answer*: "and not to touch it." She overdoes the defence. God had said "Do not eat", He did *not* say, "Do not touch." This is the first effect of the sophist's dealings: his words inspire a secret discontent which then causes us to exaggerate the severity of Divine Law. Eve continues: "Lest, that *perhaps* we should die." Just earlier she was exaggerating her defence; now, she actually lessens the threat. God, however, did *not* say, "Perhaps." He said, "The day you eat of this fruit you *will* die," – '*morte morieris*'. "Thou shalt die the death." (Gen. 2:17) - Could it be any more clearer and more formal?

Eve therefore exaggerates on the one hand and diminishes on the other. She hesitates, she falters. What gives strength to those who attack is the hesitation of those who defend themselves. At the beginning, the serpent slipped in under the modest appearance of a simple doubt and an innocent 'why'. Eve is shaken; suddenly the serpent takes the opportunity and rises up, he opposes the Divine word with the most impudent denial. '*Nequaquam morte moriemini*', - not the least in the world, he replies, "you will not die the death; for God knows that in the day you eat of this fruit, your eyes will be opened, and you will be like gods, knowing good and evil." (Gen. 3:4-5)

When talking about the 'modern idea'; one says; "the spirit of the age", or spirit of the times. And the modern idea, like the spirit of the times, is summed up in these two words: "Do not believe, do not obey. O people; now you are 'enlightened'! Knowing for yourself what is good for you and what is bad for you, you will be free, you will be independent; and each of you governing yourself, you will be sovereign, "you will be like gods" - '*Eritis sicut dii.*' (Gen. 3:5)

But, this idea is not 'modern', it is as old as the first woman; and the 'spirit of the times' is as old as the serpent who first dared to say to our first mother: "God said to you: You will die, I say: You will not die. God said; Do not eat this fruit; I say: Eat. When God speaks, do not believe; when God commands, do not obey, and you will be like gods, depending only on your own reason and your freedom."

Once again, this idea is not new. The serpent writers and the serpent orators of the 19th century invented absolutely nothing new.

Satan Exulting over Eve

The woman ate of the forbidden fruit; Adam out of complacency did the same. And their eyes, indeed, were opened. Ah! The serpent said: "You will be like gods." Good heavens! What irony!

But here comes God. The guilty ones are called forward, heard, convicted. All that remains is to strike. It must be so, because the ruling was already formally pronounced: "The day you eat of this fruit, you will die." And so, Satan trembles with an infernal joy, for now it is all over and done with this God-Man whom he was supposed to adore. But, oh what a reversal! Suddenly, God, instead of striking down guilty mankind, also turns towards the serpent and addresses him with this formidable prediction: "I will put enmities between thee and the woman, and thy seed and her seed: she shall crush thy head," - *'Ipsa conteret caput tuum.'* (Gen. 3:15)

Understand, O you who echo the serpent; hear, O you contemporary emulators of Caiaphas, Nero, Julian, Luther and Voltaire! After a century, who will count your triumphs? How many times have the likes of you declared that the kingdom and the Church of Jesus Christ are 'over'? Fools! For you, the triumph is the tomb. This Pope that you always overthrow still stands. This Church whose reign you continually declare to be forever abolished, always rises larger and stronger, right in the midst of the ruins of your ephemeral empire. Raise up, yes, proudly raise up your head causing the people to shudder at the hisses of your fury; but, act quickly: for this head of yours, which now seems so threatening and proud, I already see it crushed under the powerful heel of the Immaculate Virgin: *'Ipsa conteret caput tuum.'* - After a great crash, your very memory will have perished; and Jesus Christ still reigns. "Their memory hath perished with a noise ... but the Lord remaineth forever"- *'Periit memoria eorum cum sonitu ... Dominus in aeternum permanet.'* (Psalm 9: 7,8)

The Two Camps

Let us continue on in the Scriptures. Abel lies dead at Cain's feet. The innocent, the righteous has fallen; the traitor, the assassin triumphs.

You are weeping! You are shaking! You pity the innocent Abel! No, do not weep; no, do not tremble; no, do not pity Abel. Do not pity the martyrs — pity the Caesars. Do not pity Jesus — pity Judas, Caiphas and Pilate. Do not pity the captive of Savona; pity him who said that weapons[15] would not fall from the hands his

---

15   A reference to the captivity and exile of Pius VII under the rule of Napoleon Bonaparte. *"The Catechism Explained"* by Spirago and Clarke (1899) has an interesting paragraph that proves Fr de Boylesve's point under the sub-heading '*Of all the persecutors of the Church none have succeeded against it, and some have come to a fearful end*' (pages 235-236) - "The case of Napoleon is instructive. He kept Pius VII a prisoner for five years, he himself was a prisoner for seven years. In the castle at Fontainebleau he forced the Pope to give up the states of the Church, promising a yearly income of 2,000,000 francs; in the same place he was himself forced to sign his abdication, and received a promise of a yearly income of the same amount. Four days after giving the order to unite the States of the Church with France he lost the battles of Aspern and Erlingen. He answered the excommunication launched against him, saying the words of an old man would not make the arms (weapons) drop from the hands of his soldiers. This actually happened in his Russian campaign from the intense cold; and on the same day on which Napoleon died at St. Helena, Pius VII was celebrating his own feast day in Rome. No wonder the French have a saying: 'Whoever eats of the Pope dies.' The same fate is shared by the founders of heresies, and the enemies of religion. Arius bust asunder during a triumphal procession; Voltaire died in despair. These facts and many more of the same kind

soldiers.   Do not weep over Pius IX ... .[16] No, once again, do not pity Abel, and above all do not tremble. Do you see the man who looks distraught, pale, terrified? It is the traitor, it is the murderer, it is Cain.[17] The story of Cain is not finished!

Seth replaces Cain. Two camps are formed on the earth: that of the children of God, the sons of Seth; and that of the children of men, the sons of Cain. For a long time these two races lived separate from each other. Finally, the merger[18] between the two took

---

illustrate the words of Holy Writ: 'It is a fearful thing to fall into the hands of the living God.' (Heb. 10:31).

16   A reference to the beginning of the 'Prisoner of the Vatican' era, which began September 29, 1870 after the fall of the Rome during the Risorgimento. Bl. Pius IX was the first of the 'prisoner popes' who refused to acknowledge the new Italian government's rule over Rome and remained within the Vatican in protest. This period eventually came to an end with the signing of the Lateran Pacts on February 11, 1929, thereby establishing the Vatican City State.

17   Cain feared that anyone he would meet might kill him in punishment for killing Abel.

18   *"The sons of God seeing the daughters of men, that they were fair, took to themselves wives of all which they chose. ... Now giants were upon the earth in those days. For after the sons of God went in to the daughters of men, and they brought forth children, these are the mighty men of old, men of renown."* (Gen. 6:2,4) The Douay-Rheims bible notes that: "The descendants of Seth and Enos are here called sons of God from their religion and piety: whereas the ungodly race of Cain, who by their carnal affections lay grovelling upon the earth, are called the children of men. The unhappy consequence of the former marrying with the latter, ought to be a warning to Christians to be very circumspect in their marriages; and not to suffer themselves to be determined in their choice by their carnal passion, to the prejudice of virtue or religion." Biblical history then notes this unfortunate union brought about the race of giants who became 'famous' on the earth for their skill in warfare and earned great earthly

Cain in the Spell of Satan

renown, (see Baruch 3:26) but in spiritual terms they were so far from God and His laws to the point their corruption caused Him to wipe them out and cleanse the earth.

place. The righteous are lost the day they stop fighting against the wicked. They saw it back then. All flesh corrupted its way. The rule of empire passed to the giants, to brutal force, to famous men: "These are the mighty men of old, men of renown."- *'Isti sunt potentes a saeculo viri famosi.'* (Gen. 6:4) And God said: "I will destroy man," - *'delebo hominem'*. (Gen 6:7)

This time again, Satan triumphs: if God destroys man, He cannot come, this Son of the Woman who must crush his head.

But in the midst of this general corruption, one man remained righteous. Noah knew how to keep his family apart from the movement and ideas of his time, and he found grace before God. He receives the order to build an ark which, by saving him and his people, will be the salvation of the human race. The work lasted a hundred years, during which Noah continued to announce the terrible flood which would swallow up all men. But they ate, they drank, they built, they established themselves; and above all they laughed at the simplicity of the old man.

Just like yesterday, these powerful and famous men of today, these giants of force, smiled, calm and proud, their hands placed on their cannons, their ears stunned by the noise of universal suffrage, their eyes hovering over a prostrate multitude: for all flesh, through their dealings, had corrupted its way. At the sight of the Ark of the Second Noah, which is the Church of Jesus Christ, they shook their heads; to the warnings of the old man of the Vatican, the Pope, they responded with the sneer of Voltaire.

The Last of the Giants Destroyed

However the tide rose, and the proud inhabitants of the city of Cain fled with their baggage. The tide was still rising, and powerful and famous men were climbing the mountain. The flood was still rising, and the giants were reaching the summits. But already the waters exceed the highest peaks of the globe by fifteen cubits, covering the powerful and famous men, their great cities, their 'immortal' works; while on this ocean without a bottom and without a shore we see sailing, calm and majestic, the ark which carries the righteous. Giants, smile once again if you dare!

One righteous man, just one, was enough to save the world that was lost by the majority, by the universal suffrage of the time. "And now ... understand," - *Et nunc ... erudimini*. (Psalm 2:10)

And now educate yourselves, slaves of numbers, slaves of this foolish queen who calls herself public opinion. Dare say again that it is the majority and universal suffrage that we must ask to find where truth is and to ask what is right!

Also standing alone against all, alone against the universal suffrage of an entire people, alone against the opinion summed up in this formidable clamour: "To the cross, to the cross," - 'Tolle, tolle, crucifige', the Righteous One of Calvary in His turn will be, but in a higher order than Noah, the Saviour and Second Father of the human race.

Outside the ark of the new Noah, as long as the flood reigns, there is no salvation. This ark is the Church.

Powerful and famous men, giants of the age, you who have raised the tide of the Revolution against the Church. Take care. Remember: when the flood had passed over the earth, only Noah and those who were with him in the ark remained.

If the bloody flood of the Revolution, a mad disillusion of yours, must still yet pass over the world, beware you powerful and famous men, giants of the flesh — you will disappear under the storm; at the return of the rainbow, there will remain only the Noah of the Vatican, and those who by a sincere and complete faith will have remained with him in the Church: "Noah only remained, and they that were with him in the ark," - 'Remansit autem solus Noe, et qui cum eo erant in arca.' (Genesis 7:23)

Babel

What tower is this that rises up as if to defy the world and dares threaten a new castigating flood? A city is being built at the foot of this proud monument. Good heavens! What a movement! The work moves forward with marvellous speed. — But what has happened? Suddenly the workers stop, look at themselves, at first with a smile on their lips, then with the astonishment of stupor and fear. One person speaks, the other does not understand; this one answers, that one does not hear. Everyone speaks a new language.

These men, who just a moment ago were so united, are now nothing more than strangers to each other. The work is abandoned. This crowd, yesterday so confident, so proud, so active, today is now dividing and dispersing. This tower which was to be raised up to the very heavens and transmit the forever famous name of the builders for all ages, will be called 'Babel', which means: confusion, vanity, nothingness!

The first universal suffrage, the first plebiscite, was not successful. For having acted on their own and without a leader, this people remained a people without a name, a simple multitude, a Babel. Order only reappeared when each family grouped itself around its natural leader and thereby once again became a nation.

Noah had three sons, the second son, Cham (or Ham), had laughed at his father, and his father had cursed him.[19] Among the grandsons of the cursed man, there was one called Nimrod. This name literally means: 'Let us be rebellious', (or 'We will rebel'). We could also translate: Revolution. Without caring about the curse that has just fallen on Babel, Nimrod seizes the materials collected by the entire family and the constructions started by all the sons of Noah; he completes the first city built after the Flood and creates an empire at the very foot of the cursed tower. Nimrod is therefore, in the second phase of the human

---

19   *"And Noe, a husbandman, began to till the ground, and planted a vineyard. And drinking of the wine was made drunk, and was uncovered in his tent. Which when Cham the father of Chanaan had seen, to wit, that his father's nakedness was uncovered, he told it to his two brethren without. But Sem and Japheth put a cloak upon their shoulders, and going backward, covered the nakedness of their father: and their faces were turned away, and they saw not their father's nakedness. And Noe awaking from the wine, when he had learned what his younger son had done to him, He said: Cursed be Chanaan, a servant of servants shall he be unto his brethren."* (Gen. 9:20-25) The Douay-Rheims Bible notes that Noah did not sin here by drinking the wine unto drunkenness as he did not know the strength of the wine. The Haydock notes that it appears wine was not yet invented then, hence, his ignorance on the strength of the drink.   On interest, the Scripture mentions only Chanaan getting cursed by Noah, but, according to the notes in the Douay-Rheims edition; "The Hebrews answer, that he (Chanaan) being then a boy, was the first that saw his grandfather's nakedness, and told his father Cham of it; <u>and joined with him in laughing at it:</u> which drew upon him, rather than upon the rest of the children of Cham, this prophetical curse." But, since Cham did not help in covering his father's nakedness, and the Hebrews believed Cham also mocked Noah, he is not without fault. Therefore Fr de Boylesve obviously considered him 'cursed' as well, for having his son cursed like this by Noah is also a punishment on the father.

race after the Flood, the first powerful man on earth: "He began to be mighty on the earth" - '*Et ipse coeput potens esse in terra.*' (Gen. 10:8) He was a strong man: "he was stout" - '*et erat robustus*'; a "stout hunter": '*robustus venator*'. (Gen. 10:8) He was the first who replaced the power and authority of the father-head in the family unit with the right of force.[20]

---

20   The Douay-Rheims notes that 'stout hunter' refers not to being a hunter of animals, but of men - "whom by violence and tyranny he brought under his dominion. And such he was, not only in the opinion of men, but 'before the Lord', that is, in His sight Who cannot be deceived." That is, Nimrod's

In this he brought about a revolution, and he justified his name: he was a rebel. The monument of confounded human pride, Babel, was the capital of the first kingdom and became Babylon: "And the beginning of his kingdom was Babylon," - *'Fuit autem principium regni ejus Babylon'*. (Gen. 10:10)

Babylon will become the perpetual adversary of Jerusalem, as the Revolution will be that of the Church. Faithful to its origin, Babylon will become 'confusion', a confusion of languages and ideas, a confusion of kings and of peoples, who in turn will come to seek the rule of empire and death. It is enough to recall Nebuchadnezzar and Balthasar, Cyrus, Darius, Xerxes, Alexander, these are the kings; the Assyrians, the Persians and the Medes, the Greeks, are the peoples. Likewise, true to its name, the Revolution is nothing but the continuous overthrow of words and ideas, of rights and laws, of families and peoples.

I said 'confusion of words'; and this confusion, which at first sight seems so insignificant, generates all the others. In 1789 there was a Revolution in the name of reason, science, and in the name of the highest of sciences: philosophy - in the name of liberty, equality, and fraternity.

But 'in the name of reason' was really the flesh adoring itself under the guise of an infamous prostitute;[21] and 'in the name of revolutionary science and philosophy' was really the negation of what was

leadership acquired by brute force did not go unnoticed by God Who sees all.

21   It was reported that during the French Revolution in the midst of a 'Festival of Reason' in 1793, the revolutionaries enthroned a prostitute on the altar of Notre Dame cathedral as the 'goddess of reason'. Churches were desecrated and also turned into 'Temples of Reason'.

most capital and most certain: the negation of God, of the soul, of the other life, that is to say precisely, 'in the name of revolutionary science and philosophy' was true wisdom turned upside down and true knowledge abolished. Their 'liberty' was nothing but terror imposed by a handful of bandits on a naive people, and these proclaimed sovereign by the very people who made them their dupe and their slave; their 'equality' was only achieved through pillage and confiscation; their 'fraternity' was that of Cain, the fraternity of the assassin and the scaffold.

Let us return to the topic of Babel. Besides, we never really left it. What remains today of this proud and powerful city? Go to Babylon and see, or rather, better not go there. In the place where Babylon was, all that remains is a pile of debris serving as a den for ferocious animals and filthy reptiles. This is because Babylon must be, until the very end, the symbol of this fierce and infamous power, which we call the Revolution.

Civilization

Meanwhile, it is said that it is to the Revolution which the empire of the world and the monopoly of civilization belong. Indeed, as the name itself indicates, 'civilization' comes from 'city'. But, before the Flood, the first city was built by Cain, the first assassin, the first traitor, the first revolutionary. Shall Cain be the first 'civilizer'?

Nimrod built or at least completed the first city after the Flood, the grandson of Cham, of that same

Cham who was the first to mock authority and who was cursed by his father. Is 'civilization' to come from an insolent and cursed race?

The family of Cain and that of Cham thrive in cities. Could it be that a city offers more resources for debauchery and crime?

The patriarchs, on the contrary, live in tents and in the fields; they are shepherds. The great Moses, the liberator of Israel, is formed in the solitude of the mountains and the pastoral life. The people of God become civilized in the desert. It is in the countryside that God will ask for the liberators and the leaders of His people, the Gideons, the Jephthahs, the Samsons, the Davids. It is from the mountain that the heroic family of the Maccabees will descend. Even today, it is the man of the fields, it is the labourer, who gives a country its defenders and the Church its ministers; it is the countryside which generally produces both the soldier and the priest. The city worker rarely presents himself for the sacred militia; and often the secular militia rejects him, or, 'reforms' him, precisely because the civilization of the cities has made him incapable of the noble but harsh profession of arms.[22]

---

22   Fr de Boylesve is noting that the difference in the lifestyles of the time: those who labour in the country lived a life of hard work with little in the way of conveniences, while workers in the cities do not have a life of such hard physical labour and sacrifice as a farmer would have, for example, especially in those days. He seems to be saying here the country folk are therefore used to a life of labour and sacrifice and seem more prepared and ready follow a vocation in the religious life, the 'sacred militia', with the sacrifices that would entail. In contrast, a city person seems to shun the religious life due to the perceived sacrifices, while even a secular army finds a city person 'soft', and if they do not reject them for the army, needs to train them for combat and 'toughen them up'

Is the city the home of human corruption? We may say this when remembering the Babylon of Nimrod and of Balthasar, the Rome of the Caesars, and certain large cities of France in 1870.

On the contrary, would the simple and harsh life of the fields be the novitiate and the apprenticeship of the profession of liberator? We may say this by remembering the little people from whom the Saviour of the world came; we may still say it now when seeing Brittany and the Vendée.[23]

Civilization, as we understand it today, above all consists of the culture of the arts. There are useful arts, which constitute industry. There are creative, pleasant arts that we call the arts of pleasure. Both seem to be the prerogative of the cursed races.

Before the Flood, Jabel was the father of those who dwell in the tents: this was the luxury of the time. Tubalcain discovered the art of working bronze and iron, and even today metallurgy is the measure of a people's industry and wealth. Jubal is the father of musicians, music is the first of the arts of pleasure.

Jabel, Tubalcain and Jubal all belong to the family of the accursed, to the race of Cain.

---

in order for them to endure the hardships of war.

23   These rural areas of France refused to side with the Revolutionaries and remained loyal to the King of France and their Catholic faith. The revolutionaries were particularly brutal towards the Bretons and the Vendeans due to their loyalty, and were made to suffer horrific atrocities, the like of which could be compared with the brutality of the German concentration camps of WWII. Still, they heroically fought against the rebels and refused to renounce their faith despite threats of horrific torture and death.

After the Flood, the first nations famous for the magnificence of their cities, for the importance of their works, for industry and for commerce, came from the second accursed, I mean from Cham. Such as Misraim, who founded the kingdom of Egypt, then Chanaan, whose very name means 'merchant'. There was Sidon, who is the father of the Phoenicians, the first navigators and the first traders of the world, then finally Nimrod, the first king, the 'first great power' on earth: "he began to be mighty on the earth" - *'Inde coepit esse potens in terra'*. (Gen. 10:8)

Greece and Rome, it is true, belong to the race of Japheth; but Greece received civilization from Egypt and Phoenicia; Rome will receive its own civilization from Greece.

Today the palm of civilization, which consists of industry, well-being and power, is in the hands of three heretical peoples: England, Prussia (Germany), North America; of a schismatic people, that is Russia; and finally of a nation, which although still very Christian in number as well as in the individual zeal of its members, is nevertheless, as a political body, the figure of indifference in matters of religion.[24]

In contrast, if a people, a family, or an individual comes to distinguish themselves by their piety, their virtue, especially by their zeal for the glory of God, misfortune immediately sets out to pursue them. Remember the righteous Abel succumbing to the blows of Cain, Job atop his dunghill, Abraham not knowing

---

24 Fr de Boylesve may be referring to France here as it was still largely Catholic in number, and also the major European power at the time this book was printed in 1870, but not for long. It would soon lose this political position after the Franco-Prussian war of 1870, which brought about the unification of Germany.

where to even set up his tent, Jacob fleeing before Esau. Remember the people of Israel enslaved in Egypt, wandering in the desert, constantly oppressed by their neighbours, held captive in Babylon, and finally becoming part of the empire of the Persians, then that of the Greeks and finally that of the Romans.

Jesus Christ dies on the cross, His apostles are martyrs, His Church is drowned in blood.

If we encounter a nation famous for its faith, we can affirm in advance that, in the event of conflict with an infidel or irreligious power, the latter will defeat the former. Remember the crusades so religious and yet so unfortunate; the struggles between the priesthood and the Empire, and the persecution suffered by St. Anselm and St. Thomas of Canterbury, St. Gregory VII, Alexander III and Boniface VIII, more recently by Pius VI and Pius VII, nowadays by the innocent and virtuous Pius IX. Look at Ireland, Poland, Portugal, Spain, South America, Austria, Italy and especially Rome. All these populations, fundamentally so Catholic, are delivered to the mercy of either heresy or schism, or of a revolution worse than schism and heresy. At last, France, victorious and all-powerful as long as it fights against Catholic interests, or at least finds itself allied to heresy or paganism, such as with the English for example and with the Turks, but sees itself defeated, humiliated, crushed, as soon as it is measured against a powerful enemy of the true religion.

Truly, it seems that religion brings misfortune.

Could it be that there exists a natural and necessary incompatibility between religion and civilization? How so? If civilization consists of making men wiser, freer, more honest, more perfect, then surely it stands to reason that the agreement between it and religion is necessary and natural?

But it is not so. Why? *The civilization that they of the world propose to us is the civilization of Babel,* a material culture of force and the number of the multitude; while religion is the worship of God, and of God alone, Who alone is the Most High, Who alone is Great, Who alone is All Powerful! Whether He is represented here below by what appears to be strength or by what resembles weakness, it does not matter; the weak old man of the Vatican held captive among the brigands, (Pius IX), appears to me as great as Charlemagne on the day he was solemnly crowned Emperor of the West.

The civilization that they would like to impose on us turns minds and hearts towards the things of earth and of the times, while religion detaches souls from what attaches them and from what is happening on earth, to elevate them to God.

The civilization that is presented to us under the name of 'progress' sees nothing beyond time, while religion moves forward with its eye fixed on the future, but on an *eternal* future.

From this point we can then explain why among religious men and people there is some disdain and even neglect for any industry and for those arts whose object, using a phrase, basically a word, is the god — gold — and ultimately, the belly: "whose god is their belly" - *'Quorum Deus venter est'.* (Philippians 3:19) Daughter of the age and of the earth, the civilization of Babel has forgotten the soul and God, heaven and eternity. Daughter of heaven and eternity, Religion is too dignified to submit to an earthly civilization which is in reality only the deification of matter and the idolatry of the flesh.

Work, I know, is the condition of man here below. "Increase and multiply," said the Lord, "fill the earth, and subdue it, and rule over the fishes of the sea, and the fowls of the air, and all living creatures that move upon the earth." Religion has never stopped encouraging work. The struggle of spirit against matter, the empire of intelligence and will over the elements and over the forces of lower nature are, for man, titles of glory and signs of greatness.

Yes, truly it is. Before the Fall, work was an honour as well as an assigned duty, it has become a punishment since the Fall, and an expiation and a reparation as well as a necessity. For it was said to man, "By the sweat of your brow you shall eat your bread."

No, the Church does not condemn industry, because industry is intelligent work. In fact, far from it, the Church has blessings both for the works of man and for the fruits that his labour obtains from the earth.

But if God said, "Subdue the earth and subdue the animals," He did not say, "Subdue man to the earth, subdue man to the animal." Nowhere did God say to man, "Thou shalt be the slave of gold, thou shalt be the slave of the senses." Now, there is a civilization which is nothing but the overthrow of human dignity, the subjugation of intelligence to matter, the enslavement of liberty to the senses and the passions. Religion cannot be reconciled with *that* kind of civilization.

God said to man, "Subdue the earth and rule over the animals," but nowhere did He say, "Rule over man and subdue him." However, there are men, and they are the most miserable in every respect, who impose themselves on their equals; and, what is even more pitiful, there are men who, forgetting their dignity and abdicating their freedom, allow themselves to be dominated by a handful of libertine sophists, who with a breath, they could drive them into the ground.

They say to me that this tyranny from the one and this servitude from the other do not constitute the normal and usual situation of society; these audacities on the one hand and such cowardice on the other are peculiar to *revolutions*, and that revolution only passes away, taking with it the villains who were its authors and the fools who were its naive admirers, and also those inert men who were its auxiliaries, its slaves and ultimately its victims.

I know it; but there is another tyranny and another servitude which seems to constitute the constant state of society. On one hand, it is a rich and powerful minority which takes its repose and enjoys itself, on the other hand there is a poor majority which works and suffers to satisfy the ever increasing greed of the rich and the never-ending baseness and ever more greedy luxury of the idle libertine.

Then we are told: "Look and see: this nation, this city, Paris, for example, or London, where the most appalling poverty crawls at the feet of the most disdainful opulence: this is 'civilization'."

Religion, I recognize, speaks a different language and presents a different type.

To the rich she says: "Why always hoard?" - "Fool" - '*Stulte*',- this night your soul will be required of you, and for whom will these goods be? Give to the poor, give to Lazarus who is suffering and dying of hunger; otherwise your sepulchre will be hell: "he was buried in hell" - *'Sepultus est in inferno'*. (Luke 16:22)[25]

Then, turning towards the poor man, Religion says to him: "Patience: one day work will be replaced by rest, and pain by joy. The hard work, the miseries and the sufferings of this life will end, but your rest and the joy will not end. Blessed are the poor, not because civilization here below can change the earth into a paradise, but because the kingdom of heaven belongs by right to those who despise not the rich but riches, and to those who are poor or who become voluntary poor: "Blessed are the poor in spirit" - *'Beati pauperes spiritu.'* (Matt. 5:3)

Get out of there, leave it, the civilization of Babylon. It is on the one hand the tyranny of the rich, on the other the slavery of the poor; it is pride on one side, it is jealousy on the other side, both always growing, and permanently constituting the Revolution.

So let us return to the first moments of human existence. There I see and hear God establishing the family and with it paternal royalty. But I do not know

---

25   Fr de Boylesve has combined two parables here: the first is the parable of he the rich hoarder who planned to build bigger storehouses and live off his surplus when his fields produced abundantly, forgetting the tithes that were meant for the poor and the Temple. *"Thou fool, this night do they require thy soul of thee: and whose shall those things be which thou hast provided. So is he that layeth up treasure for himself, and is not rich towards God."* (Luke 12: 21-22) The second parable is of Lazarus, poor man, and Dives a rich man. Dives was sent to hell for refusing to help Lazarus, while Lazarus was saved.

that he authorized Nimrod,[26] and I do not think He blessed Babel.

The man whom God calls after the Deluge to form a people, Abraham, will be a *father*, and the people coming from him will be a *family*. Also they will be the people of God. Now, in the countries that are offered to us these day as a example of civilization, we see too much of Nimrod and Babel.

If it is permissible to give words their legitimate meaning, we must call 'civilization' that which makes men 'civil', that is to say 'sociable', in a word, what unites them together. Men unite through intelligence and will. Intelligences can and only truly agree in truth; wills can only truly agree in what is good. What then is the 'truth' which remains in the minds of these men who no longer recognize the immortal soul nor God; and what 'good' can they want? Material good, sensual good, the type of good that an animal seeks. Is mindless stupidity the civilization that the men of 1789 and 1870 claim to impose? Such was the civilization of the human family at the time preceding the Deluge: all flesh then had corrupted its way; such will be the civilization of the world at the moment which will come before the universal conflagration; such was still the

---

26   While all authority comes from God, as Our Lord even told Pilate the pagan governor he was given authority over Him for that moment in judgement as authority comes from Above, there is God's absolute Will and permissive Will: Fr de Boylesve seems to be showing the difference here in that God had ordained (authorized) and blessed the paternal rule in the family beginning with Adam and Eve, while there is no evidence of Nimrod receiving such a blessing, Nimrod seized a tyrannical rule himself, which God permitted, but obviously was not a blessed rule as we see from the fruit thereof.

civilization at the time when the race of Cham held the sceptre by the hand of Nimrod and Canaan.

Then, to the corruption of the flesh, which was even more frightful than before the Deluge, is added the corruption of the spirit. Slave of his passions and senses, man stoops down even to that which is most inferior to him. He sees a god in an animal, in a plant, in a piece of wood, marble or metal that his hand has just shaped. Egypt, so sombre and grave, in all seriousness idiotically prostrates itself before the vegetables of its gardens, before the animals of its houses, before the monsters from its river. The learned Chaldea falls on her knees before the sun, before the statue of her king, and before a hideous serpent. Soon genius and strength, raised to their highest power in Greece and in Rome, will bow before inert idols, inanimate works of a mortal artist. In a word, as Bossuet said so well, everything is God, except God Himself.

The Great Nation

From the heavens God looks down on this deluge of errors and vices. He is looking for another Noah to build a new ark of which the first was only a symbol and which itself will be the figure of an even more perfect ark of salvation. This time God wants a living ark, a family, or rather, an entire people whose mission will be to cross the waves of the indolent and impure world, and to preserve the blessed seed of this Son of the Woman who must crush the head of the serpent.

His eye was fixed on Abraham. "Go forth out of thy country," He said to him, "and from thy kindred, and out of thy father's house, and come into the land which I shall show thee. And I will make of thee a great nation, and I will bless thee, and magnify thy name ... and in thee shall all the kindred of the earth be blessed." - *'In te benedicentur omnes cognationes terrae.'* (Genesis 12:1-3)

Having left Chaldea by divine order, Abraham will pitch his tent in the middle of the cursed race of Canaan. It seems that God delights in making the faith of the righteous shine through the dark contrast with what surrounds them.

However, where is this great people of which Abraham must be the father? Sarah his wife is barren, he himself is advanced in age: all hope is lost. But the man of faith persists in hope: "(Abraham) who against hope believed in hope" - *'Contra spem in spem credidit.'* (Rom. 4:18).

The growth and prosperity of the impious makes you impatient for justice! For example, there is a people who date their greatness from the time when they abjured their faith to give in to worship gold, throwing themselves at the feet of an impure tyrant (Henry VIII) and then a shameless and bloodthirsty queen (Elizabeth I). There is also a State (Germany) whose existence dates back to an apostate (Luther), who to free himself from his vow of chastity became a Protestant, and since then, has continued to grow through crime at the expense of the Catholic powers. Continuing on, there is a nation which only became significant since the time when its Czar became its pope, (schismatic Russia) and one would say that its strength grows with its fierceness against Catholic

Poland. Beyond the seas, it is a new people who reach their peak through a civilization without religion or morality. (USA)[27]

However, "God is patient because He is eternal" - *'patiens, quia aeternus'* (St. Augustine).[28] The centuries belong to Him, because He is the King: "The king of ages ... immortal," - *'Regi saeculorum immortali'*. (1 Tim. 1:17) So do not be in a hurry for justice. Wait until these 'happy' and proud nations have filled the measure. Who knows? Perhaps even now he is ready, the man whom God has chosen to be able to justify His Providence, and who is destined to confound at the same time both those whom His patience scandalises and those whom it encourages.[29]

Do you see this old man sitting quietly in his tent? Who would recognize in this peaceful shepherd the father of a nation whose empire will one day

---

27   I.e. the separation of Church and State must be referred to here = a civilization without an official religion. Also, the right to the 'pursuit of happiness' more often than not leads to the pursuit of immoral pleasures of an earth-bound happiness, and rarely to a spiritual life.

28   St. Augustine explaining verse 9 of (2 Peter 3): The Lord delayeth not his promise, as some imagine, but dealeth patiently for your sake, not willing that any should perish, but that all should return to penance."

29   As we see in Biblical history, God raises up chosen souls to turn around the tide of evil and to bring about His justice. Fr de Boylesve notes there may be a predestined soul waiting in the wings so to speak for these modern ages and who will confound those scandalised by God's patience and His seeming 'slowness' in punishing the wicked nations, and, also confound those who are 'encouraged' by this delay, i.e. those misusing the time of God's patience to grow more in evil rather than repent and return to Him. We cannot help but suspect that Fr de Boylesve may have been hinting to the Great Catholic Monarch and Angelic Pontiff prophecies with this observation.

replace that of the Canaans, the Pharaohs and the Nebuchadnezzars of all countries and all ages? Yet today, the Son of this old man, the descendant of Abraham, is the King of peoples and kings.

Walk in the presence of God, believe His word, hope against hope; then wait. You are one of those whom the All Powerful uses to break the force of the godless, and to save the people.

At last, he is born, this long-awaited and promised son. And already the lovable Isaac is the joy and the glory of his father. But God calls Abraham. "Here I am," replies the old man. "Take your son," said the Lord, "your only son, your beloved son, your Isaac, and offer him to Me as a burnt offering on the mountain." Abraham, without saying anything, obeyed immediately. Arriving at the foot of the mountain, he loads the sacrificial wood onto the shoulders of the innocent Isaac. He himself sets the fire which must consume the victim, and the knife which must immolate him. The son even helps his father build the altar and set up the pyre. Everything is ready; Isaac's gaze seems to seek the victim, and he meets a look from his father that he understands. He immediately places himself on the wood and lets himself be tied to it. Abraham stretches out his hand, he takes the sacrificial knife, he is about to strike. God calls him a second time: "Abraham, Abraham!" - "Here I am," replies the old man – "Lay not your hand on the child," continues the Voice from above. "I have sworn to Myself," continues the Lord, "because you have done this, and because of Me you have not spared your only

The Sacrifice of Abraham

son, I will bless you, I will multiply your race like the stars of the sky and like the sands of the sea. In your race will all the tribes of the earth be blessed."

Cross over eighteen centuries since then and see. On the slopes of a mountain, another Isaac climbs, burdened down, He too with the wood on which He must be immolated. This time, it is not a father who accompanies Him, it is a Mother. It is true that she does not carry the knife of sacrifice, she herself will not raise a hand against her Son to strike Him, but instead she will stand and witness the cruel torture and the long agony of this only and beloved Son, because this time the angel will not come to stop the blow, and Jesus will expire in the most atrocious pain before the eyes of His Mother.

Weep: for once again, all is lost. This only Son was precisely this offspring of Abraham and Isaac in whom and through whom all nations were to be blessed. He is dead, weep ... .

No, do not weep! The cross only seemed to be the end of His reign as well as of His life – instead, the cross became His royal standard, and through the cross He conquered the world. Who can count the children whom Abraham became the father of through the death of Jesus? Who can speak about the number of believers? You would sooner have counted the stars that shine in the sky or the grains of sand that line the ocean!

Before, outside of Israel, no one knew the names of Abraham and of Isaac. Today, thanks to Jesus, these two names are great, glorious and blessed. All those who bless Abraham in the person of his Son Jesus are blessed. Those who curse Him are cursed. And, with the exception of the peoples who persist in rejecting

the messengers of this Son of Abraham, there is not a tribe in the world that has not received in Jesus the promised blessing: "And in thy seed shall all the nations of the earth be blessed,"- 'et benedicentur in semine tuo omnes gentes terrae.' (Genesis 22:18)

Thus, through Jesus, Abraham becomes the founder of a great nation: "And I will make of thee a great nation"- 'faciamque te in gentem magnam.' (Genesis 12:2) Where is the empire which, by extent, by force, by power, by duration, is comparable to the empire of this Son of Abraham, the Church of Jesus Christ?

Measure its extent. Empires, kingdoms, republics have their limits; the Church does not know of any. Its extent is the circumference of the globe: "You shall be witnesses unto Me ... and even to the uttermost part of the earth," - 'eritis mihi testes ... usque ad ultimum terrae'. (Acts of the Apostles 1:8)

You say: "But the Church is in the State." Indeed, the Church is in the State, but as with the air is in this room which it fills and which it exceeds at the same time; as also with the light that is both in your eye which it illuminates and in all eyes open to receive it. Thus the Church is in France and beyond; in Europe and beyond. The Church must be in the State since it must reign over all men and over all nations: "Teach ye all nations:" - 'docete omnes gentes,' (Matt. 28:19), since it needs be everywhere: "even to the uttermost part of the earth"- 'usque ad ultimum terrae' (Acts 1:8); and that consequently, within its limits, it contains all the States at the same time as it exceeds each of them. If it is therefore true that the Church is in the State, it is even more true that the State is in the

Church: "And I will make of thee a great nation," - *'Faciamque te in gentem magnam'.*

Often an empire loses in strength what it gains in territorial extent; for the Church this law is different.

There is not an earthly throne that has not ended up collapsing into the dust or the mire. Where are the monarchies of those strong men who were called Sesostris, Assur, Nimrod, Nebuchadnezzar, Cyrus, Alexander, Caesar? What is the fate today of those countries or those dominating cities that are called Egypt, Nineveh, Babylon, Persia, Greece or Rome? Only one throne of the Son of Abraham, only one Empire laughs at the flow of centuries: it is the Church of Jesus: "And I will make of thee a great nation"- *'Faciamque te in gentum magnam'.*

The power of *this* Empire corresponds to its strength *and* its extent.

We say of certain nations: 'the great powers, the high powers'; but, however high and great they may be, these powers stop at the surface; they only touch upon the earth and the body. The Church alone has the power to reach the mind and the heart; it alone can impose its rule on the intelligence and the will. For to it alone it was said: "Teach", behold, we see the rule of empire over the intelligences; to it alone was it said: "Teaching them to observe all things whatsoever I have commanded you", (Matt. 28:20) that is the dominion over wills. To the Church, therefore, and to it alone belongs the royalty of souls. Therefore it alone, the Church, is the great power, the great nation: "And I will make of thee a great nation"- *'Faciamque te in gentum magnam'.*

Religion Enthroned

Endowed with such an extent, strength and power, this empire is established for an immortal duration.

All empires have a beginning, and all, one after the other come to an end and pass away. Eternal as the Word, the empire promised to Abraham will continue for eternity: "and itself shall stand for ever" - *'et ipsum stabit in aeternum'* (Daniel 2:44), for this empire is the kingdom of heaven: *'regnum caelorum.'* It will last on this earth for as long as the stars will turn. For Jesus said to his messengers: "Behold I am with you ... even to the consummation of the world," -' *Ecce ego vobiscum sum ... usque ad consummationem saeculi'.* (Matt. 28:20). His reign will know no end: "And of his kingdom there shall be no end" - *'et regni ejus non erit finis'*, (Luke 1:33). The Lord will reign throughout eternity and beyond: "The Lord shall reign for ever and ever ," - *'Dominus regnabit in aeternum et ultra'.* (Exodus 15:18)

Look and see: by extent, by force, by power and duration, the Church contains and dominates all nations, all states, without any of them being able to contain or stop it, support it or dominate it. It is the fulfilment of the promise made to believers by the Father: "I will make you a great nation," - *'faciamque te in gentem magnam'.* Thus is justified the invincible hope of this man of faith who "hoped against all hope" - *'contra spem in spem credidit'.* (Romans 4:18). We too, I believe, have reason to hope. Our hope rests on a past which guarantees the future, even when it should be, so it seems, in despair of the attacks of hell and its human minions.[30]

---

30   Fr de Boylesve was writing a note of encouragement here – France was on the cusp of the Franco-Prussian war,

He will Supplant

Esau, careless and flippant, sold his birthright for a dish of lentils. Jacob, industrious and regulated, was true to his name and 'supplanted' his brother. 'Jacob' means: 'he will supplant'.[31]   As a result, Esau threatens Jacob's life.

The princes and the great ones of the world, thinking only of their pleasures, have lost their influence over the people. Only Jesus Christ, through His Church and through His Vicar, can save the world today. Esau swore the death of Jacob, but it is in vain:

invasion from a Protestant force, and, Rome and the Vatican were under attack by the anti-religious liberation forces of Italy. While all seems hopeless for the state of the Church and Catholic nations due to the fury of Hell's followers on earth attacking from every side, the faithful will always have God's never-failing promise that the Church will last forever, Christ's kingdom will never end. The same is as true today as it was then: even when it would seem we should be in despair by how bad and godless things appear to be on earth, we, like Abraham, can hope against hope. God is faithful. The Church will stand until the end of time.

31   Esau and Jacob were twins, and, fought even while in the womb. Their mother Rachel prayed for an answer and the Lord told her this struggle meant: "Two nations are in thy womb, and two peoples shall be divided out of thy womb, and one people shall overcome the other, and the elder shall serve the younger." (Gen. 25:23) Esau was born first, and was red and hairy: Esau therefore means 'hairy'.   Jacob was born holding on to Esau's heel, therefore, 'Jacob' means, "holder of the heel" or "supplanter", because he twice deprived his brother of his rights as the firstborn son. "Rightly is his name called Jacob; for he hath supplanted me lo this second time", (Gen 27:36)

Jacob will always supplant Esau. (Same with the world that attempts to crush the Church). The Church will always dominate the world, which can only be saved by it; the Pope will always be higher and more powerful than the prince, who without the Pope, will be the plaything of the people. The Pope will be more powerful than the people, who without him, will become the prey of the prince.

However, in the meantime, Jacob flees his brother. So later will a future Son of Jacob flee the wrath of a son of Esau — this future Son will flee the Idumean Herod. Retreat or flight encourages the enemy and discourages friends, and even when it is a tactical feint, a ruse of war, it almost always seems an admission of inferiority. So the one fleeing hardly leaves without feeling something of sadness and discouragement. But God is pleased to raise up the lowly when they are humble, and when humiliation has engendered humility. For, on the first night of his pilgrimage, Jacob will be encouraged by a wonderful dream.

Lying on the sand, his head resting on a stone, with no other defence and no other wealth than his travelling staff, the heir of heavenly promises and blessings slept peacefully. During his sleep he saw an immense ladder with the base resting on the earth and the top reaching to the heavens. The angels went up and down the steps of this marvellous ladder, and God leaned on the top. "I Am," said the Lord to the fugitive, "I Am the God of Abraham and of Isaac. ... Thy seed shall be as the dust of the earth: thou shalt spread abroad to the west, and to the east, and to the north, and to the south: and in thee and thy seed all the tribes of the earth shall be blessed." (Genesis 28:12-14)

The mystical ladder first represents the material world of which each atom as well as each star that was created is a degree by which God descends to us by making Himself known and loved, by which we must ascend to God through knowledge and through love.

This ladder also represents Mary. Through her, God descends to us by becoming man within her. Through this ladder, Mary, we go back to Jesus, and also through Jesus, Who is our Mediator, we go back to the heavenly Father. This ladder represents Divinity descending to humanity, and at the same time raises humanity up to the Divinity.

Finally, this ladder also represents the Church. Through the Church, and through the Church alone, God sends down His Word and His grace upon us. Through the Church, and through the Church alone, man ascends back to God. Through the Church, the earth touches heaven. Also, it is only through the Church of Jesus Christ that the race of Jacob covers the ground like dust, extending from east to west and from north to south, bringing the celestial blessing to all the tribes of the earth.

Everything in the history of Jacob announces the Saviour. Rachel and Lia, these two sisters who became the spouses of the patriarch and who cost him so many years of hard labour, recall the two peoples of God; the synagogue and the Church, both of which Jesus united through the hard work of His Passion and of His Cross, thereby joining in His Person the two Testaments, the Old and the New. "Who hath made both one" - *'Qui fecit utraque unum'*, (Ephesians 2:14).

Jacob returns to his father, but he still fears Esau's anger. Along the way, he fights against God by wrestling with the angel, and, through the constancy of his prayer, strong against the Almighty Himself, he obtains what he asked for, and, he manages to appease his brother's resentment.

Jesus, preparing to return to His Father, struggles in the Garden of Gethsemane and also perseveres in prayer: "And being in an agony, He prayed the longer," - '*Factus in agonia prolixius orabat*'. (Luke 22:43) Strong against the all-mighty and all-righteous wrath of a vengeful God, the Second Israel obtains the reconciliation of men with God and also with each other.

Who can speak of the pain of Jacob when he mourns his son Joseph, this beloved son whom a cruel beast, that is, whom jealousy devoured? In comparison, who can speak of the pain of Jesus, when He sheds not only tears, but all His Blood, for so many souls so dear to Him, which hell and the world never cease in their attempts to steal away from the tenderness of His Heart? Who can count the tears and the drops of Blood shed by the Saviour, when, casting a glance into the future from the height of His cross, He saw the Eldest Daughter of His Sacred Heart, (France), devoured by the cruel monster of revolutionary impiety and sold to a foreign barbarian; when He saw His beloved Vicar also sold and reduced to the condition of a prisoner?[32] However, let us be reassured: Joseph left the prison, and Jacob was able to see him again in all the splendour of grandeur. Thus so will it be the Church and France: one through the other and one with the other, they will emerge from the ordeal more powerful and more glorious than ever, because Jesus Christ must triumph, reign and dominate through

---

32   Fr de Boylesve is again speaking of the events of his times: the Franco-Prussian war and the siege of Rome.

France, His Eldest Daughter: "Christ conquers, Christ reigns, Christ commands," - *'Christus vincit, Christus regnat, Christus imperat'*.[33]

The Lion of Judah

Jacob is about to die. He summons his sons together to announce to them their destiny. After severe reproaches addressed to the first three sons, Reuben, Simeon and Levi, he then comes to Judah, and seized with a divine enthusiasm, he cries out: "Judah, your brothers will praise you." (Gen. 49:8) Indeed, after the death of Joshua, it is the tribe of Judah that God designates to march before Israel against the Canaanite. David, the honour and the glory of Israel, will be a son of Judah. So also will be He of Whom the angel will say: "He shall be great " - *'Hic erit magnus'* (Luke 1:32) - the great *par*

---

33   *"Christus vincit ..."*; from the hymn, "Laudes Regiæ", or "The Royal Praises" at solemn events, such as the inauguration of a pope, or, in centuries past, at the coronation of the Holy Roman Emperor.

"Eldest Daughter of the Church": since the time of the conversion and coronation of Clovis I, the first King of France, France became known as the 'Eldest Daughter of the Church' and was the defender of Catholic Christendom and the papacy. Again, we may see evidence here that Fr Marin de Boylesve may have believed in the Great Catholic Monarch and Angelic Pontiff prophecies that foretell a King of France will rise up, re-establish the Holy Roman Empire, and restore both the world and the Church one last time in union with a saintly pontiff before the arrival of the Antichrist. See footnote 29.

Judah

excellence, He will be a son of David and of Judah. "Judah, thee shall thy brethren praise" - *'Judah, te laudabunt fratres tui'*.

"Thy hands shall be on the necks of thy enemies" - *'Manus tua in cervicibus inimicorum tuorum'*. (Gen. 49:8)   See how everything bends under the strong hand of David, son of Judah!   Philistines, Syrians, people of Moab, Ammon, Amalek, Edom, so many perpetual adversaries of the people of God who are all reduced to submitting to the yoke. "Thy hands shall be on the necks of thy enemies"- *'Manus tua in cervicibus inimicorum tuorum'*.

There is another Son of Judah.   From the wisdom of His words, from the power of His action, it was easy to recognize Him as the Messiah. His Jewish brothers misunderstood Him.   Their nation is over. Scattered throughout the world, they attest to all peoples and all ages the strength of the Hand that weighs on their heads: "Thy hands shall be on the necks of thy enemies"- *'Manus tua in cervicibus inimicorum tuorum'*.

The Caesars and the pagan peoples rushed upon the envoys of the Son of Judah. They delivered them to irons, to fire, to wild beasts: where are the Caesars and the persecuting people today? The Hand of the Son of Judah crushed them. "Thy hands shall be on the necks of thy enemies"- *'Manus tua in cervicibus inimicorum tuorum'*.

Where are these great and formidable heresies with which proud and indocile geniuses used as a pretext to oppose the Word of the Son of Judah? The Empire supported them with all its might; and their triumph was, it seems, assured.   But, by clashing against the Church of Jesus Christ, the Empire became the Late Empire:[34] "Thy hands shall be on the necks of thy enemies"- *'Manus tua in cervicibus inimicorum tuorum'*.

Go ahead and charge forth, you barbarians of the North and barbarians of the South; go ahead and unite violence and voluptuousness to conquer and seduce. You will not succeed in the end. Before the Vicar of Jesus Christ, Attila the Hun retreated; in front of one of his ministers, the proud sicamber[35] Clovis bowed his head. The fanaticism of Mohammed succumbed under the hand of the Popes, the lieutenants of Jesus Christ, and under the hand of the Christian kings, His disciples.[36] "Thy hands shall be on the necks of thy

---

34 'Heresies' – Fr. De Boylesve may have been referring to the great heresy of Arianism here which was horrifically strong at this time, with few opposing it. 'Late Empire' – a period referring to the crisis period in the Roman Empire, generally beginning with the rule of the notorious persecutor Diocletian in 284 AD and the establishment of the Tetrarchy in 293 AD by him, to the death of Heraclius in 641 AD. This period saw the rise of Constantine and the legalization of Christianity, and the condemnation of the Arian heresy.

35 'Sicamber' – a member of the Sicambri, a Germanic people who during Roman times lived on the east bank of the river Rhine, in what is now Germany, near the border with the Netherlands. By the 3rd century, the region in which they and their neighbours had lived had become part of the territory of the Franks, which would later become known as France. In poetry, 'Sicambri' became a term used to describe the Franks (French). An example of this custom is recalled by St. Gregory of Tours who stated that on the occasion of his baptism into the Catholic faith, Clovis I was addressed as a Sicamber by St. Remigius, the officiating bishop of Rheims. At the crucial moment of Clovis' baptism, Remigius declared, "Bend down your head, you proud Sicamber. Honour what you have burnt. Burn what you have honoured."

enemies"- *'Manus tua in cervicibus inimicorum tuorum'*.

Go ahead unite your efforts, political and legal; combine the artifice of laws and the force of arms to dominate and enslave the Church of the Son of Judah. Your laws are nothing but cobwebs; your weapons, blades of straw. The Hand that lifts you up, O kings; the Hand that frees you, O peoples, this Hand will fall on your rebellious heads and will chastise you, one by one. "Thy hands shall be on the necks of thy enemies"- *'Manus tua in cervicibus inimicorum tuorum'*.

And you, men of the antireligious and antisocial Revolution, you have broken the yoke that troubled the wayward liberty of your heart even more than that of your mind; and then in the name of 'liberty', you have outlawed all liberty, except the liberty of error and vice. But your fury will only serve to bring back the strength of the Hand the Son of Judah, which has already fallen on your heads: "Thy hands shall be on the necks of thy enemies"- *'Manus tua in cervicibus inimicorum tuorum'*.

Jacob's prophetic blessing on Judah continues: "The sons of thy father shall bow down to thee. " (Gen. 49:8)

"Judah is a lion's whelp: to the prey, my son, thou art gone up: - *'Catulus leonis Juda : ad praedam, fili mi, ascendisti.'* (Gen. 49:9)   I know Jesus, Son of Judah, is the Lamb of God; but He is also the Lion. See how He rushes to snatch from the roaring lion of hell the prey of souls that sin had delivered to its fury!

____

36   No doubt a reference to the Christian reconquest of Europe, driving back the invading Islamic armies.

"Resting thou hast couched as a lion, and as a lioness, who shall rouse him?" - *'Requiescens accumbuisti ut leo et quasi leoena; quis suscitabit eum?'* (Gen. 49:9)

He lay first on the cross, then, in the tomb. It is the *lion's* rest; during this fearful rest, everything trembles. Who would dare wake Him?

When the Pharisees and the Scribes, when the politicians and the sophists line up against the Church, we tremble.   But, it is not *our* place to tremble! The lion sleeps, but it is the *lion's* repose.

Up to now, the patriarch Jacob has spoken in figurative language, he will next take a prophetic, historical tone.

"The sceptre shall not be taken away from Judah, nor a ruler from his thigh, till he come that is to be sent, and he shall be the expectation of nations." - *'Non auferetur sceptrum de Juda, et dux de femore ejus, donec veniat qui mittendus est, et ipse erit expectatio gentium.'* (Gen. 49: 10)

Jacob speaks of Him Who is to be sent as of a person already promised and expected: "he that *is to be sent"* - *'Qui mittends est.'* We see that it pertains to this Son of Abraham, of Isaac and of Jacob himself, in Whom all the tribes of the earth must be blessed, with this Son of the Woman by whom the head of the serpent must be crushed.

"He shall be the expectation of nations" - *'et ipse erit exspectatio gentium'*. Among all peoples we find, although some more or less altered, the tradition which recalls the promise of a Saviour. Moreover, the people specially chosen to preserve faith in the Messiah and to give this faith to the world, the people of Israel, will find themselves in contact with all civilized and civilizing peoples, with all peoples that commerce or ambition will bring to bear through all corners of the globe. Such as the Egyptians, the Phoenicians, the Assyrians, the Persians, the Medes, the Greeks and finally the Romans. Thus, the whole world will know that there exists a people that was founded solely on the expectation of an extraordinary Person Who must save and dominate all nations. "He shall be the expectation of nations" - *'Et ipse erit exspectatio gentium.'*

This prophecy is clearer than all the previous ones. It assumes and confirms them. Not only does it indicate in advance the One Who is to be sent, "he who is to be sent" - *'qui mittends est'*; but it marks the time *when* He will come: it will be when the people of God will no longer be governed by a son of Judah. "The sceptre shall not be taken away from Judah nor a ruler from his thigh, <u>till</u> he come that is to be sent, *'Non auferetur sceptrum de Judah ... donec veniat qui mittendes est.'* So as long as the family of Jacob did not form a people, as long as it did not have a son of Judah as its leader, the Messiah did not come. But as soon as Judah has received the sceptre, which will be done by the election of David, Judah will retain it until the coming of the promised Saviour. Thus, even during the dispersion and the captivity of Babylon, the people of God, then reduced to the sole tribe of Judah, govern themselves by themselves. Susanna's trial shows Judah exercising the highest right of sovereignty, the right of life and death.[37] There will come a time when this tribe

---

37 The tribe of Judah was allowed to govern the captive people of Israel and appoint judges, they could even impose the death penalty according to Jewish law as we see from the

is no longer governed by leaders drawn from its own ranks: then, will the One appear Who is to be sent and Who is awaited by the nations.

History in fact teaches us that at the moment when the sceptre fell from the hand of Judah and into that of the Idumean Herod and the Roman people, there came a Son of David, a Son of Judah, Who was to pick up the fallen sceptre and wield it over all the nations. This Child was called Jesus; His sceptre is a cross: the Cross holds dominion over the world.

Jacob adds that Judah will: "tie his colt to the vine and his donkey to the vine." (Gen. 49:11)   The vine represents the people of God. We see in Isaiah (5:4)[38] the Lord complains of the ingratitude of His vineyard: "What should I have done for my vineyard that I have not done?" This vineyard is the Jewish people. "For the vineyard of the Lord of hosts is the house of Israel," - *Vinea enim Domini exercituum domus Israel est,*' (Isaiah 5:7)   Jesus Christ, in the parable of the vineyard, uses the same comparison to designate this same people.[39] — The vine, *'vitis'*,

---

history of Susanna and the corrupt judges who tried to seduce her, and then have her wrongfully accused of adultery when she refused so she would face the death penalty. The prophet Daniel held an investigation and discovered their evil plot: Susanna was found innocent and the evil judges were sentenced to death instead for bearing false witness.

38   Fr de Boylesve mistakenly attributed this to Jeremiah. I have corrected it to Isaiah.

39   Isaiah in this passage speaks of the Lord preparing His vineyard, by building a wall, picking out the stones, planting the best vines, and also building a watch tower in it, but, the fruit it yields turns out to be wild and bitter, and so, after all that preparation, the Lord is angry, declaring what more could he have done for this vineyard to make it fruitful? - *"What should I have done for my vineyard that I have not done?"*

designates the Saviour, Who declared Himself the vine: "I am the true vine," - 'Ego sum vitis vera.' (John 15:1) —The donkey that we find with the colt: we see this fulfilled on the day of the triumphal entry of Jesus into Jerusalem.[40] The donkey represents the synagogue, the ancient people of God who were long accustomed to the yoke of the law; the untamed colt

---

And so, it will be laid waste, a prophecy of the Jews turning away from God and the punishment they will receive. Christ also uses a parallel parable to show this prophecy in Isaiah represented the rejection of the prophets sent to the people of Israel through the centuries, then, ultimately, the rejection of Him as the Messiah, after which the 'vineyard' would finally be given to a new people, the Gentiles, who would accept Him and give Him the promised fruit of conversion: *"And he began to speak to the people this parable: A certain man planted a vineyard, and let it out to husbandmen: and he was abroad for a long time. And at the season he sent a servant to the husbandmen, that they should give him of the fruit of the vineyard. Who, beating him, sent him away empty. And again he sent another servant. But they beat him also, and treating him reproachfully, sent him away empty. And again he sent the third: and they wounded him also, and cast him out. Then the lord of the vineyard said: What shall I do? I will send my beloved son: it may be, when they see him, they will reverence him. Whom when the husbandmen saw, they thought within themselves, saying: This is the heir, let us kill him, that the inheritance may be ours. So casting him out of the vineyard, they killed him. What therefore will the lord of the vineyard do to them? He will come, and will destroy these husbandmen, and will give the vineyard to others."* (Luke 20: 9-16)

40   "And when they drew nigh to Jerusalem ... Jesus sent two disciples, saying to them: Go ye into the village that is over against you, and immediately you shall find an ass tied, and a colt with her: loose them and bring them to me. ... Now all this was done that it might be fulfilled which was spoken by the prophet, saying: Tell ye the daughter of Sion: Behold thy king cometh to thee, meek, and sitting upon an ass, and a colt

the foal of her that is used to the yoke." (Matt. 21:1-5) The
prophecy referred to is in Zachariah (9:9): "*Rejoice greatly, O
daughter of Sion, shout for joy, O daughter of Jerusalem:
behold thy king will come to thee, the just and saviour: he is
poor, and riding upon an ass, and upon a colt the foal of an
ass.*"

represents the pagan peoples who barely know the law and know no constraint.

Judah tying the foal to the vine represents Jesus joining and attaching the pagan nations represented by the untamed colt, to the ancient people of God, who are represented by the vine: "Tying his foal to the vineyard" - *'ligans ad vineam pullum suum.'* (Gen. 49: 11) Judah then linking the donkey to the vine represents Jesus, Who after having declared Himself the vine: *'Ego sum vitis,'* attached to Himself the ancient synagogue, the ancient people of God, in the person of His apostles and first disciples, all of whom were children of Israel.

But this union does not come about without a fight. The donkey resists — the synagogue refuses to unite with Jesus Christ. The fiery colt rears up — the pagan peoples only submit to the Christian yoke after having overthrown and trampled in their own blood the envoys whom the Master had sent and who were charged with the task of taming them.

Also see the Son of Judah: His robe and coat are red with blood. "He will wash his robe in wine," said Jacob, "and his garment in the blood of the grape." (Gen. 49:11) Here, you recognize the Eucharistic wine changed to the Blood of Jesus by the virtue of the consecration. It is in this Blood that the robe of the Saviour is washed and purified; *'lavabit in vino stolam suam'*. This garment, it is the Church. In the blood of the grape you recognize the Blood of Jesus flowing under the whip, under the crown of thorns, and through the openings of His hands, His feet, and especially in His Sacred Heart — it is this Precious Blood in which the royal mantle of the Saviour is washed and consecrated; this mantle is the priesthood;

"And his garment in the blood of the grape,"- *'Et in sanguine uvae pallium suum'*. (Gen. 49:11)

Jacob continues: "His eyes are more beautiful than wine, and his teeth whiter than milk." (Gen. 49: 12) The eye represents intelligence, the wine recalls the blood. Blood is the life of the body, while intelligence is the life of the soul and is superior: "His eyes are more beautiful than wine," - *'Pulchriores sunt ocul ejus vino.'*

Teeth, by which we grasp the nourishment of the body, can represent the will by which we grasp that which is good, that is, the nourishment of the soul. Milk recalls the first and main food we receive. Teeth symbolize strength, while milk signifies sweetness. Thereby joining gentleness to strength, Jesus by His invincible will seizes the pagan nations who barely possess the first elements of moral life, and He unites them and incorporates them by His grace, especially through Holy Communion which sanctifies them. However, the brilliance of His Holiness always remains infinitely superior to the candour of the innocence to which He restored to them: "and his teeth whiter than milk,"- *'Et dentes ejus candidiores lacte.'*

These are the blessings Jacob prophetically pronounces on Judah. Everything announces victory and royalty.

I shall conclude here with Joseph, the beloved son of Jacob who was sold by his brothers, thrown into prison by slander, but free and master even when under slavery and thrown into prison, eventually leaving the dungeon to sit in the foremost palace near to the king, destined to save both the Egyptians whose slave he once was and the jealous brothers who sold him. By these features we recognize Him Who the

Heavenly Father calls His Beloved Son, Who, sold by one of His own for the same sum as Joseph, was delivered to foreigners by His brothers, slandered against, condemned to the tortuous death reserved for the slave. However, free and Master even in the prison of death, He emerges triumphant from the sepulchre and goes to sit at the right hand of the Heavenly Father. By virtue of the omnipotence which He received from Him, He saved and nourished both the Gentiles to whom He was delivered and His brothers by whom He was sold. He makes Himself the food of hungry souls, their source of Life, and like Joseph of the Old Testament, He gradually submits to Himself the whole earth, all the nations to the true Pharaoh, to the true King of the whole world.

Whoever the person is in Scripture who prophetically represents Jesus, it is always the Kingdom which they announce and represent in advance.

Pharaoh

Soon the family of Israel multiplied in Egypt in a prodigious way. The Pharaoh of that latter time did not know Joseph, the son of Jacob to whom Egypt owed its salvation and to whom the kings of Egypt owed the progress of their power. This new Pharaoh said to his people: "Behold the people of the children of Israel are numerous and stronger than we. Come, let us wisely oppress them." (Exodus 1:10)

Israel here represents the Church. This Pharaoh who does not know Joseph reminds us of certain kings and rulers who have forgotten that it is to Jesus Christ and His Vicar that princes owe this power, to that paternal and strong office of which the Christian monarchies alone have offered the authentic model. The new Pharaohs of these times grow concerned about the ever-increasing number of the children of the Church, and in turn they say to the people: "Come, let us skilfully crush this Church which, by its example and its lessons, hinders and condemns our passions."

We must study the policies of the Pharaohs. Always and everywhere, before and after Jesus Christ, in Europe as in Egypt, this policy is the same.

They know that a people bent under material work forgets heaven and eternity, the immortal soul and God, to think only of earthly things, things of the times and of the flesh. They know that a people thus degraded is an enslaved people. Also, see how they turn all intelligence and all strength towards earthly matter! Hear them exalting material and sensual well-being above all truly productive industry and commerce! And now they rule: a docile troop moves at their feet under the harsh work of mortar and brick: "And they made their life bitter with hard works in clay, and brick, and with all manner of service, wherewith they were *overcharged* in the works of the earth." - '*Atque ad amaritudinem perducebant vitam eorum operibus duris luti et lateris, omnique famulatu, quo in terrae operibus premebantur.*' (Exodus 1:14) Crushing the spirit under matter — such is the first secret of the oppressor's crafty wisdom.

Their second secret is even more clever. The ancient Pharaoh ordered all male children to be thrown into the Nile: a sure and quick way to put an end to a people. The process of the new Pharaohs is no less certain. A flood of impious teaching and immoral education is spread over a country; the youth loses their spiritual intelligence and their heart. These spiritless youths, as long they agree that the new Pharaoh of the times surpasses the old, they will never become a people. But, here comes Moses, who stands before Pharaoh.

<u>Moses</u>

Hear what the Lord God of Israel says: "Let my people go that they may offer sacrifice unto me in the desert." (Exodus 5:1)   The Pharaohs are not accustomed to being addressed in this strong language. "Who is the Lord," replies the Pharaoh of Egypt? '*Quis est Dominus*'.   "I know not the Lord." - '*Nescio Dominum*.' Indeed, you will know Him.

Plagues then follow upon plagues. A mere gnat has put an end to the power of Pharaoh's magicians. Surely they must finally recognize the finger of God; but the proud Egyptian does not surrender. The plagues continue. "Leave," then said the tyrant; "but only the men will go." (Exodus 10:11) However, Moses is not about to make concessions, he is not of that school.

Moses and Aaron before Pharaoh

"We will leave," said the old man, "us, our wives, our sons and our daughters, with our flocks." Moses does not give in, but Pharaoh persists. The plagues resume their course. "Leave," Pharaoh finally cries, "but leave your flocks." Politics, it seems, would attempt to have Moses bend to another compromise, that the deliverance of his people needed to be purchased at the price of a sacrifice, a sacrifice light in comparison with the servitude and the oppression they were under. But, Moses understands nothing about human politics, he will not sell out what God has declared theirs. "All the flocks will go with us," replies the old shepherd, "and not even a hoof will remain," - *'Non remanebit ex eis ungula.'* (Exodus 10:26) Moses gives the example! Grant nothing to error; do not give up anything of the truth, *not one syllable, not one iota.* Remember St. Athanasius and Basil the Great, the St. Anslems and the St. Thomas Beckets of history, the Gregory VIIs and the Pius IXs. Beware of the soft and yet useless negotiations of a policy which calls itself 'liberal' when it is nothing but base enslavement. Despise this false moderation, which, under the guise of religious liberty, shows itself gentle and easy-going towards the enemies of faith while at the same time reserves nothing but proud harshness and ferocity for the defenders of the Church and the Pope.

The wise men of Israel once fell into this baseness. As slaves, they tremble at the feet of Pharaoh, and they only regain their elevated manner of language through Moses when he stands for them. This man of God will save them despite their servile timidity. They will leave with their children and their old men, with their wives and their daughters, with their brothers and their sheep.

They will leave theland of slavery, taking with them the spoils of Egypt, just wages for their long and hard labours.

But now, going back on his word, Pharaoh sets out in pursuit of the Hebrews with his horsemen and his chariots. Israel trembles and murmurs. We can agree that at this moment they are not without cause. Caught between Pharaoh's army on the one hand, and the Red Sea on the other, these unfortunate people believe they are lost without hope. Yet, always, and especially at the moment of anguish, we forget that God is waiting for the admission of our weakness that He may reveal Himself. Pharaoh triumphs, Israel despairs — but Moses raises his rod. The waves open, Israel passes through. Pharaoh, it is true, pursues his prey to the very heart of the half-open sea, but rest assured: Moses raises his rod a second time, and suddenly the suspended waves fall like a storm on Pharaoh's chariots. The oppressor had said: "I will pursue and overtake him," - *'persequar et comprehendam.'* (Exodus 15:9) With a mere breath God overwhelms him, Israel is free.

Children of the new people of God, at the sight of these waves of these times which rise like mountains, fear has seized you. O men of little faith, rest assured: it is a path that the Divine breath is preparing. It is not for *you* to fear, it is for the Pharaohs to tremble. Just wait a little longer, and you will know it.

How All the Pharaohs End Up

"Let us sing to the Lord," cries Moses, "for He is gloriously magnified,"- *'Cantemus Domino: gloriose enim magnificatus est'*; (Exodus 15:1). Let us sing: let us praise loudly, let us praise with all our strength Him Who alone is the Lord. Where are these timid or ungrateful souls who claim to impose silence on us, who do not allow us to proclaim loudly the truth, the whole truth, the rights of God and of His Church? God manifested His greatness. What do you have to fear? — Pharaoh? — His power has become the plaything of the waves.

God manifested His greatness, and how? By saving the weak, and by having the strong lost. Do you hear this, you politicians who place greatness and glory in following and serving Pharaoh, that is to say, the strength of force, whether 'Pharaoh' and 'force' be a king or a people, the will of one individual or the opinion of the crowd, whether it is what you call 'personal government' or 'universal suffrage'? You pity the servility of the little and great ones of yesteryear in the face of Caesars and kings; allow *us* to pity the servility that prostrates *you* at the feet of a no less capricious and even more tyrannical queen who calls herself 'opinion' or 'the multitude'. (Democracy.) Caesar, at least from one point of view represented Divine authority, and in bowing before him, even though his name was Nero, it really was before God that the brow was bowed. But *your* idol, oh! *She* is not in the Vatican, *she is in the street*; in vain do I search for a divine trait in her, I only discover the vulgar and common; she is not even Pharaoh, she is public opinion; she is not even a voice, not even an articulate sound, but a confused noise, unintelligible as well as unintelligent, in a word, the noise of the crowd.[41] (Babel).

Understand then, finally, O you who call yourself a man of independence and liberty, understand that true greatness consists in saving oppressed weakness, and in declaring oneself boldly against Pharaoh and Egypt, against the world and the prince of the world, against public opinion and against the kings of public opinion. "Let us sing to the Lord: for he is gloriously magnified, the horse and the rider he hath thrown into the sea." - *'Cantemus Domino: gloriose enim mafnificatus est; equum et ascensorem dejecit in mare.'* (Exodus 15:1)

The horse represents the people, simple and docile under the hand of their rider, their Pharaoh. Behold, Pharaoh has launched his steeds, his people against Israel, which today means against the Church, and at the sight of Pharaoh now, in the face of 'public opinion', you tremble and you claim to impose your fears on us? But we do not tremble, for God will still cast both the steed and the rider into the sea. My

---

41   Apparently, Fr de Boylesve is comparing secular, anti-religious and anti-Church democratic republics with a 'woman of the street', the 'great whore of Babylon' in scripture, in particular, the Masonic Republic that overthrew the Catholic monarchy of France during the Revolution. Those who leave God's laws were referred to as having committed 'fornication' and 'adultery' against Him in the Old Testament and was a grievous as practicing witchcraft. Christ's kingdom and the Church in the New Testament is compared to His bride, the 'Heavenly Jerusalem', while Satan's reign, particularly through the Antichrist, is symbolized by the 'Whore of Babylon'.

strength is in God alone; it is God alone Whom I praise and exalt, I have only contempt and pity for these great ones and for these forces which terrify you and which, despite your fear of them, you never cease to praise.

"The Lord is my strength and my praise," - *'Fortitudo et laus mea Dominus.'* (Exodus 15:2) It is from God and not from Pharaoh that I await salvation and freedom; "And he is become salvation to me. He is my God,"- *'Et factus est mihi in salutem. Iste Deus meus.'* (Exodus 15:2) This is my God; let yours then be Pharaoh, may yours be, once again, this idol that we call 'public opinion'. Go ahead, praise, celebrate what the world praises and celebrates, I will only praise God; "He is my God and I will glorify him," - *'Iste Deus meus, et glorificabo eum.'* "He is the God of my father," (Exodus 15:2) - the God of Abraham, Who is the father of believers; the God of my father, that is also, the God of the Pope, the father of Christians. He defended the father, He saved the children; He overwhelmed Pharaoh, He overwhelmed Caesar. Neither Egypt with its Pharaohs, nor Rome with its Caesars, nor despotism, nor the Revolution could lose the people that His arm defended; I will therefore exalt Him, and I will exalt only Him; for He alone is the Most High. "God of my father, and I will exalt him," - *'Deus patris mei, et exaltabo eum'.*

How has the God of my father shown Himself? In that He did not remain indifferent to the misfortunes of the children, and that He rose to defend them: "The Lord is as a man of war," - *'Dominus quai vir pugnator.'* (Exodus 15:3)

Away with the so-called peacemaker, so meek and benign in the face of the ungodly and the wicked; away with the 'man of peace' who compromises and sits with a smile on his lips in the assembly of the enemies of the Church.

"We are too weak," you say, "we are too few! See; strength and number are on the side of Pharaoh." I know it, so I will count neither on my strength, nor on the number of my comrades-in-arms in the fight. My hope is in God. Look, God is called the Almighty: "Almighty is his name," - *'Omnipotens nomen ejus'*. (Exodus 15:3)

Are you asking for proof? Look again: surrounded by his chariots and his army, Pharaoh seems to you the personification of strength and power. A little longer, and it will be all over for Israel. O Moses, why have you angered this great king and this formidable people? What a reckless old man! In order to find such a similar disregard for the apparent conventions of wisdom and politics, we see the Old Man of the Vatican bringing together in a Council all the leaders of the people of God, almost as if to deliver them all together in one go to the furies of the Revolution.[42] You even believe it is so, and following with your eyes the rapid chariots of the Pharaoh of these times, you tremble for Israel. But behold, God takes both the chariots and the army of the mighty of the earth, and throws them all together into the depths of the waters; "Pharaoh's chariots and his army he hath cast into the sea," - *'Currus Pharaonis et exercitum ejus projecit in mare.'* (Exodus 15: 4) It is the same idea now as it was then at the beginning. But what do see happening in this image? It was already a great feat to throw the horse and the rider into the sea: "The horse and the rider he hath thrown into the sea," -

---

42   A reference to Bl. Pius IX convening the First Vatican Council on December 8, 1869, right in the midst of the upheavals of the anti-clerical Risorgimento.

'*Equum et ascensorem dejecit in mare.*' (Exodus 15:1) But a whole army of chariots and warriors! ... What strength! What power! And, the Divine Warrior does not limit Himself to precipitating them, throwing them down from top to bottom, '*dejecit*'. Such is the strength of His arm that, seizing all the chariots and the entire army at the same time, He casts it a considerable length into the middle of the waves; '*projecit*'. Furthermore, these chariots and these warriors were led by the king's first captains; "His chosen captains" - '*Electi principles ejus.*' (Exodus 15:4) There were also other elite princes, the Neros and the Julians, the Ariuses and the Pelagiuses, the German Caesars and the English kings of the Middle Ages, the great 'reformers', the so-called philosophers, and the revolutionary immortals of 1789. '*Electi principles ejus.*' But what can we say of those who today call themselves: 'science' – 'knowledge'! Science, in a mere *person*? What then do we think of those they call 'the *power*'? Science, and the great powers of the 19th century, are far from having the greatness of the Pharaohs of yesteryear. But even if they were greater, and even if they exceeded them by head and chest, it would only be a mere game for the Most High to submerge them in the waves of the Red Sea; the "chosen captains are drowned in the Red Sea". (Exodus 15:4) It is no longer only in the sea that they are submerged, it is in the *Red* Sea, in a sea of blood figured in advance by the very colour that the algae gave to the waters of this formidable area of the ocean.

"The abysses have covered them." Literally, the depths of the whirlpools have become their clothing;

The Egyptians Drown in the Sea

an image of the impious, who, by rushing into crime, have made it a garment, a habit, a covering: "The abysses have covered them."- '*Abyssi operuerunt eos*'. (Exodus 15:5)

"They are sunk to the bottom like a stone." (Exodus 15:5) From the height of his power the enemy of the Church is thrown into the depths of impotence, and his fall is accelerated like that of a stone thrown from top to bottom. We cannot help but recognize here as an example the man who, at the very moment when he held the Pope in his victorious claws, suddenly saw the weapons fall from the hands of his soldiers, and was himself thrown onto a barren rock in the heart of the ocean.[43] Yesterday the most powerful kings trembled at the mere sound of his name; today under the care of a simple officer who serves as his jailer, this great, this formidable, this all-powerful one of the earth has descended alive into the depths: "they are sunk to the bottom like a stone," - '*descenderunt in profundum quasi lapis.*' (Exodus 5:15) And so the divinely inspired cantor sings of the greatness of God, which never shines with more glory than in the ruin of those who rise against His designs: "Thy right hand, O Lord, is magnified in strength: thy right hand, O Lord, hath slain the enemy." - '*Dextera tua. Domine, magnificata est in fortitudine, dextera tua, Domine, percussit inimicum.*' (Exodus 15:6) "And in the multitude of thy glory thou hast put down thy adversaries," - '*Et in multitudine gloria tuae deposuisti adversarios tuos.*' (Exodus 15:7) A double lesson is here: one to address of proud who rise up against the Church — God strikes them and places them at the bottom of the abyss. The other lesson is addressed to the conciliators who dream of nothing but peace by making an alliance with the oppressors of truth and justice, a concession with the persecutors of the Church and the priesthood. God does not know how to be so tolerant towards those who are themselves so intolerant towards His people. Against them he unleashes the breath of His anger, and this breath carries away the 'mighty' impious and devours them like a blade of straw: "thou hast sent thy wrath,

---

43   Another reference to Napoleon Bonaparte. See footnote 15 regarding his downfall.

which hath devoured them like stubble." - '*Misisti iram tuam, quae devoravit eos sicut stipulam.*' (Exodus 15:7)

In this third depiction of Divine triumph, the gradation of scale is perceptible. In the first, we saw that it is the horse and rider thrown into the sea. In the second, the entire army and all the chariots are launched out into the middle of the waves and fall to the depths of the abyss like a stone. Now, in the third scene, the anger of God increases, while His triumph at the same time is now more complete, more terrible, and even depicted as effortless. One breath, just that, and the proud enemy is devoured like chaff in the fire.

Under this breath of Divine wrath the waters gathered together and the wave stopped its restless, mobile nature, held firm in an accumulation, while the abysses (literally the whirlpools) of waters froze and remained unshakeable within the sea itself.

And so, under Divine action, the nations mobile like the waters, and revolutions terrible like whirlpools, are stopped, immobilized as if frozen under the impression of an unknown force. Then, the people of God, the Church, pass through. With the voice of its Moses, the voice of the Old Man of the Vatican, the Council (Vatican I) assembles and continues its work; "And with the blast of thy anger the waters were gathered together: the flowing water stood ..." - '*Et in spiritu furoris tui congregatae sunt aquae : stetit unda fluens ...*' (Exodus 15:8) (Hebrew. '*steterunt in cumulum flentia*',) "... the depths were gathered together in the midst of the sea." - '*... congregata sunt abyssi in medio mari,*' (Hebrew. '*aestus*', the whirlpools, '*caogulati, con gelati sunt*'). (Exodus 15:8)

But, the waters are to shortly resume their formidable mobility. Listen and watch.

"The enemy said: I will pursue and overtake, I will divide the spoils, my soul shall have its fill: I will draw my sword, my hand shall slay them." (Exodus 15:9) What will God do to oppose this so proud and threatening language? Just a breath: "Thy wind blew," - '*flavit spiritus tuus*', (Exodus 15:10) and suddenly the sea covers and envelops them as clothing seizes the body of man: "... and the sea covered them," - '*Et operuit eos mare*' (Hebr. 'vestivit'.) (Exodus, ibid.) Now when Pharaoh's warriors fall into the depths, it is no longer described 'like stone' — it is like lead; "they sunk as lead in the mighty waters," - '*submersi sunt quasi plumbum in aquis vehementibus*'. (Exodus, ibid.) At this point, Moses no longer knows in what terms to extol the power of the God of Israel. "Who is like to thee, among the strong, O Lord," he cries? '*Quis similis tui in fortius, Domine?*' (Exodus 15:11). Jewish authors assure that these words from the song of Moses were adopted as a motto by Judas, son of Matthias. The hero would have inscribed on his flag the first syllable of the three Hebrew words: 'Who is like you among the gods?' In Hebrew; '*mi*' (or '*ma*') '*camacah beloïm*': MA-CA-BE. This would be the origin of the glorious nickname of Judas MACHABEUS, the meaning of which would thus recall the very name of the Archangel Michael, in Hebrew MI-CHA-EL – which means, 'Who is like unto God'?

Let this be our motto: let it be a cry of gratitude for the triumphs already won; let it be a cry of confidence for the battles that await us.

In memory of the numerous victories of the Church over the series of submerged Pharaohs of history, in the sight of the new Pharaohs who draw the sword and who cry: "I will pursue, I will seize" -'*Persequar et comprehendam*'; let us repeat with Moses: "Who is like to thee, among the strong, O Lord? Who is like to thee, glorious in holiness, terrible and praiseworthy, doing wonders?" - '*Quis similis tui fortibus, Domine? Quis similis tui, magnificus in sanctitate, terribilis atque laudabilis, faciens mirabilia?*' (Exodus 15:11)

These are the titles which declare the excellence and superiority of God. Holiness, first of all, the specific character of which is not being able to suffer sin, a character directly opposed to that of the present age that is so tolerant, so indifferent towards error and vice, and thereby is so small, so worthless, so helpless. Do you want to truly be great? Aspire to do great things: *be holy*, have a hatred and a horror of sin, error and vice: "glorious in holiness" - '*Magnificus in sanctitate.*' (Exodus 15:11)   Only those who were terrible against the crafty sophists and the wicked became great. Even the pagan myth here agrees with the Bible: Hercules became raised up to the level of a god because he was terrible to cruel and pernicious monsters. The historical hero of Greek pagan history, Alexander, was great because he was terrible to the enemies of his homeland, and true to the meaning of his name, he was the 'defender', the 'help' of 'strong men' against the effeminate tyrants of the East. The great man of the Old Testament, Moses, was the deliverer of Israel because he was terrible with his mighty rod. Finally, the One Who will be the Great *par excellence*; "He will be great"- '*hic erit magnus*', (Luke 1:32) will be so precisely because He will show Himself terrible to the universal oppressor of the human race: "Glorious in holiness, terrible and praiseworthy, doing wonders,"- '*Magnificus in sanctitate, terribilis et laudabilis faciens mirabilia.*' (Exodus 15:11) He has only contempt for those timid and cowardly souls who retreat before the enemy, especially for those who seek to come to compromising terms, a lukewarm middle ground between Moses and with Pharaoh, between both Jesus Christ and with Belial, with both the Church and with the Revolution, with both Peter and with Caesar, between those men who with the sons of the crusaders call themselves Catholics, and the sons of Voltaire who declare themselves liberals.[44]

But what are the wonders wrought by the Lord? And why does He not have His equal among the strong? It simply is enough for Him to stretch out His hand, and suddenly the earth devours the enemies of His people: "Thou stretchedst forth thy hand, and the

---

[44]   Even the Lord declares in Revelation He cannot abide those who will take the middle ground under a false peace in order to sit contented on this earth, and do not truly work at advancing in the spiritual life, thinking they are fine as they are: *"I know thy works, that thou art neither cold, nor hot. I would thou wert cold, or hot. But because thou art lukewarm, and neither cold, nor hot, I will begin to vomit thee out of my mouth Because thou sayest: I am rich, and made wealthy, and have need of nothing: and knowest not, that thou art wretched, and miserable, and poor, and blind, and naked. I counsel thee to buy of me gold fire tried, that thou mayest be made rich; and mayest be clothed in white garments, and that the shame of thy nakedness may not appear; and anoint thy eyes with eyesalve, that thou mayest see."* (Apocalypse 3:15-18) We must be as gold tried tried and purified in the fire, rejecting the world and its pomps if we wish to be His followers. God would rather us grow rich with eternal riches—virtue and wisdom—which takes spiritual toil, entails sacrifice, and requires a zealous will determined to persevere through the help of God as we cannot accomplish perfection ourselves.

earth swallowed them." - *'Extendisti manum tuam et devoravit eos terra'*. (Exodus 15:12)

Now, why these prodigies of strength?   The mighty of the earth display their strength against the weak: the Lord displays His Power against the strong and for the weak: "In thy mercy thou hast been a leader to the people which thou hast redeemed," - *'Dux futisti I misericordia tua populo quem redemisti.'* (Gen. 15:13) It is not enough for Your Mercy to guide and lead Your people; in Your strength You carry them to Your holy habitation.   As much as you are terrible against the enemies of Your people, you are as good and tender towards Your children; "And in thy strength thou hast carried them to thy holy habitation." - *'Et portasti eum in fortitudine tua as habitaculum sanctuam tuum.'* (Gen. 15:13)

With a glance while crossing the desert, Moses sees the nations rising against Israel: "Nations rose up, and were angry" - *'Ascenderunt populi et irati sunt'*. (Exodus 15:14)   Thus, after the passage through another Red Sea, after having crossed the sea of His own Blood, after the triumph of His resurrection, Jesus saw the people and the kings rise up against His Church and shaking with anger. At this sight He said to His Apostles; "Go, teach ye all the nations ... you will be My witnesses to the ends of the earth ... I am with you all days until the consummation of the world. ... Courage, I have conquered the world." - *'Confidite, ego vici mundum'*. (Matt. 28:19.   Acts 1:8.   Matt. 28:20. John 16:33)

See how already the pains of childbirth have seized the Philistines; the princes of Edom were troubled, the forts of Moab trembled, the inhabitants of Canaan became stiff and motionless. (Exodus 15:14-15)

Such is it still today. Even as I meditate on these lines, such is the attitude of the Caesars and the great, the politicians and the powerful who have posed themselves as adversaries of the Church currently assembled in council (Vatican I) to establish the reign of Jesus Christ throughout the earth.

Complete your work, O Lord. Let it no longer be simply by a breath; may it no longer be Your hand only, but let it be Your entire arm that extends over Your enemies, and may terror and fear fall upon them: "Let fear and dread fall upon them, in the greatness of thy arm: let them become unmoveable as a stone, until thy people, O Lord, pass by: until this thy people pass by, which thou hast possessed." - *'Irruat super eos formido et pavor, in magnitudine brachii tui : fiant immobiles quasi lapis, donec pertranseat populus tuus, Domine, donec pertranseat populus tuus iste, quem possedisti.'* (Exodus 15:16) It was a prayer in the mouth of Moses, and it was also a prophecy. This prayer is still a prophecy, and its fulfilment is already beginning before our eyes — Refer back to June 1870.[45]

They were surprised at the immobility of the powers of this world, they only spoke of wars and revolutions; and the war did not break out, and the revolution stopped. We looked for the cause of this stupor which kept the world in suspense and we found a thousand causes: but there was only one. The people of God had to pass: it was to give them time, it was to allow the Council to crown its leader with the halo of infallibility that the kings remained fixed in this

---

45   A reference again to the upheavals in France and Italy at the time just as Bl. Pius IX was about to convene Vatican I. See the next footnote.

surprising immobility, and that these almighty people of the earth were reduced to impotence.[46] "Let them become unmoveable as a stone, until thy people, O Lord, pass by: until this thy people pass by, which thou hast possessed." - *'Fiant immobile quasi lapis donec pertranseat populus tuus, Domine, donec pertranseat populus tuus iste, quem possedisti.'* They will arrive at their destination; God Himself is responsible for giving

---

[46] In the few years leading up to 1870, France and Prussia were chomping on the bit to enter into war with each other. Meanwhile, the Risorgimento was raging in Italy, the anti-clerical Garibaldi and his revolutionaries were determined to capture Rome as it was agreed the unification of Italy would not be complete without it. However, even before the Council was summoned in June of 1868, the revolutionaries were stopped in their tracks from advancing upon the Eternal City thanks to the Papal Zouaves and the French forces of Napoleon III who had agreed to protect the Papal States. An important victory for the Papal States was the battle of Mentana in 1867. The Papal Zouaves and a French battalion clashed with Garibaldi's red shirt volunteers headed to Tivoli after initially having failed to take Rome when the Romans did not revolt and join their cause as had been expected. The victory of the Franco-Papal Zouaves at Mentana gave the Papal States three more years, and allowed Bl. Pius IX to convene the First Vatican Council and declare the dogma of papal infallibility. In fact, Fr de Boylesve mentions in his book *"The First and Second Joseph"* an interesting account of a miracle attributed to St. Joseph regarding the protection of Jesuit property near Tivoli during the battle of Mentana. Fr de Boylesve obviously saw such miraculous protection as proof that heavenly intervention must have indeed kept the revolutionaries from advancing upon Rome for a time. (See part 17 – 'The Garibaldians and the Jesuits' in the book *"The First and Second Joseph"*). Unfortunately, The Franco-Prussian war broke out and Napoleon III was forced to recall his French troops, allowing the revolutionaries the opportunity to finally seize the city. However, not until the Council had declared upon papal infallibility.

to Israel the empire of the Promised Land, that is, giving empire over the nations to the Church, giving empire to the faithful soul over their passions, and finally empire to all Heaven: "Thou shalt bring them in," -'*Introduces eos.*' It will not be temporary, but solid and permanent: "And plant them in the mountain of thy inheritance,"- '*Et plantabis*'. (Exodus 15:17)

Israel is only a small people, and yet it will occupy the summit of ancient history; the great peoples of the civilization of that time, the Assyrians, the Persians, the Greeks and the Romans, will only be the pedestal of the people of God, who, in the end, will dominate all the remnants of human empires through this Son of Abraham, of Isaac and of Jacob, of Judah and of David Who must take possession of the nations as an inheritance, and Whose reign must be immortal and universal: "And plant them in the mountain of thy inheritance," - '*Et plantabis in monte haereditatis tuae*'.

There on this summit, at this height which surpasses both the heights of science, and the heights of power, surpassing the most sublime philosophers and the proudest potentates, the Lord has prepared a dwelling, He has built a sanctuary that all human and infernal forces cannot shake. "You are Peter," He said, "and on this rock I will build My Church." Who are you, O men, who are you, wise of a day, who are you, O powerful ones of yesterday, to overthrow an edifice that God Himself built? "Thy most firm habitation which thou hast made, O Lord," - '*Firmisimo habitaculo tuo quod operatus es, Domine.' (Exodus 15:17)* Who are you to tear down a sanctuary that the Divine Hand has fortified? "Thy sanctuary, O Lord, which thy hands have established." -'*Sanctuarium tuum, Domine, quod firmaverunt manus tuae.'* (Exodus 15:17)

Nations and kings, why do you shake with anger? Powerful ones and sages of the world, why do you unite your strength and intrigues? God wants to reign over Israel, and through Israel over the world, that is, God wants to reign over the Church, and through the Church over the nations. A God Who so easily destroys His proud enemies in the waves will reign when He wants, where He wants, as long as He wants.   Now, He wants to reign in time, He wants to reign on this earth, He wants to reign everywhere, He wants to reign forever, and He will reign: "The Lord shall reign for ever and ever." - *'Dominus regnabit in aeternum et ultra.'* (Exodus 15:18)

The Lord will reign for eternity and *beyond*: "forever and beyond" - ' *in aeternum et <u>ultra</u>'*. What a sublime hyperbole. Although it is impossible, suppose for example's sake that there was a limit to eternity and that there is a point 'beyond' it; in this 'beyond' God would still reign. How? Listen to the evidence Moses gives. "For Pharaoh went in on horseback with his chariots and horsemen into the sea: and the Lord brought back upon them the waters of the sea: but the children of Israel walked on dry ground in the midst thereof." (Exodus 15:19) God, Who can thus play with the sea and its waves, also plays with time and the ages. He is All Powerful, Infinite, Eternal, and if He wants to reign, it needs be He must reign; but since He does desire it, it *will* be done. Know this, Pharaohs of all countries and all times, the Lord, the Christ, by His Church, will reign in time and in eternity and beyond: *'Dominus regnabit in aeternum et ultra.'*

How Revolutions End Up

The revolutionaries cry: *All* men are equal, *all* are holy, *'omnis multitudo sanctorum est.'* This is the programme, this is the declaration of Core, Dathan and Abiron: "And when they had stood up against Moses and Aaron, they said: Let it be enough for you, that all the multitude consisteth of holy ones, and the Lord is among them: Why lift you up yourselves above the people of the Lord?" (Numbers 16:3)[47]   No more master, no more prince, no more priest. *Everyone* is the master, the prince, the priest. The sovereign God resides in each member of the multitude, *"The Lord is among them," - 'et in ipsis est Dominus.'*

It is true that the princes were imprudent enough to claim that they were only responsible to God and their sword, but then the people followed suit and said: I too rely only on God and my sword, "The Lord is among them",- *'in ipsis est Dominus.'* The people cry: perhaps each of us individually would be less strong than you; but we are a whole multitude of sovereigns. Is your person sacred? Ours too: "all the multitude consisteth of holy ones," - *'quia omnis multitudo sanctorum est.'* Combined, our swords are well worth as much as yours. Why then, and by what right, do you elevate yourself above the people who too belong to the Lord - *'cur elevamini super populum Domini".*   Here we see, the theory of the independence and sovereignty

---

47   "And behold Core ... and Dathan and Abiron ... rose up against Moses, and with them two hundred and fifty others of the children of Israel, leading men of the synagogue, and who in the time of assembly were called by name." (Numbers 16: 1-2)

of the multitudes is not new: it is, basically, only a variant of the formula of the Cores, the Dathans and the Abirons: "All the multitude consisteth of holy ones," - *'quia omnis multitudo sanctorum est'*.

Certainly all men are equal in the sense that all are endowed with reason and free will; all are composed of a body and a soul; all are sons of the same father, and therefore brothers; all are the work and image of the same God. All are holy, if not in fact, at least by right: for all *needs* be consecrated to God by baptism, all are required to show themselves worthy of the God Who created them, worthy of the God Who saved them, "all the multitude consisteth of holy ones, and the Lord is among them," - *'omnis multitudo sanctorum est, and in ipsis est Dominus.'*

Apart from this, all men are 'similar' rather than 'equal', because there are no two men equal in intelligence and energy, no two are equal in strength of soul or strength of body, no two are equal in vice or virtue. Were we all equal, there would still exist between us a subordination and a distinction which would make some above others. God is free to distribute His gifts as He pleases. Furthermore, to first give us natural life according to our nature, then, to give us the life of supernatural grace, it pleased Him to use the assistance of some of our peers or our equals whose mission it is to represent and to exercise His superior authority.

It was through your parents that He gave you existence, through them that He preserved your childhood. Recognize in them that they are the representatives and ministers of the authority of Him Who is *par excellence* the Father, and from Whom all paternity flows: "For this cause I bow my knees to the

Father of our Lord Jesus Christ, of whom all paternity in heaven and earth is named," - *'ex quo omnis paternitas'*. (Ephesians 3:15)

It is through the prince that God assures you the peaceful enjoyment of this life and temporal goods. Recognize in him that he is the representative of the Power and the minister of the Providence of Him Who alone gives and regulates power, "Let every soul be subject to higher powers: for there is no power but from God: and those that are, are ordained of God," - *'non est potestas nisi a Deo, quae autem sunt, a Deo ordinatae sunt.'* (Romans 13:1)

It is through the priest that God communicates the supernatural life to you, that He maintains it, restores it and increases it in your soul. Recognize in him the representative of Jesus Christ, the minister of His power and His mercy, for Jesus Christ Himself said to His Apostles: "He who hears you, hears me; he who despises you despises me," - *'qui vos audit, me audit; qui vos spernit, me spernit.'* (Luke 10:6)

Do not reproach your father, do not reproach the prince, do not reproach the priest, do not rebel against the superiority of rank they occupy in relation to you and the authority they exercise over you. Do not reproach them for raising themselves above you, it was God Himself Who raised them. If there is anyone who raises their head too proudly it could well be *you!* "You take too much upon yourself," - *'multum erigimini'*! (Numbers 16:7). Yes, you are too proud, too haughty, you and this inert and servile crowd, whom you have seduced and subjugated, for it is against the Lord Himself that you have risen, "and all thy company stands against the Lord," - *'et omnis globus tuus stat contra Dominum.'* (Numbers 16:11)

The Death of Core, Dathan and Abiron

"For what, indeed, is Aaron, that you would murmur against him?" -'*quid est enim Aaron, ut murmuretis contra eum*'. (Numbers 16:11) A man, a man like you, a man who is perhaps inferior to you in genius, in character, in virtue; but be careful: this man was nevertheless chosen by God to represent and exercise His authority. — So, you are so proud and dignified that you cannot bring yourself to obey an equal, to bow before a man? At least that is what you say. In fact, however, you recognise the representative of the people, the chosen one of the multitude as a superior! Come on then, you are less proud than you say you are, and above all, you are less free than you think. Slave to popular majority, that is to say of force, and of the least intelligent force, you obey *only* man. For my part, if I am prouder, more dignified and more independent than you, if I respect my parents, the prince and the priest, and if I obey them, it is because I recognize them to be the representatives of God — I obey *God*, not anyone else.

We know how the insurrection of Core and his accomplices ended. The fire of Divine wrath enveloped them; "The earth broke asunder under their feet: and opening her mouth, devoured them with their tents and all their substance. And they went down alive into hell the ground closing upon them, and they perished from among the people." (Numbers 16: 31-33) We know this, and we are frightened by the threatening pride of the new Cores of these days. Look then and see: the ground is already undermined under their feet, the spark is ready, just a little more longer, and you will see them swallowed up with all that they possess.

Such is the history of all revolutions. Thus end all the Cores, all the Dathans and all the Abirons!

The Star of Jacob

Israel advances towards the Promised Land. As it approaches, Balac, king of Moab, grows afraid. He summons a famous soothsayer named Balaam and urges him to curse the people of God. But, overcome by a spirit superior to that which ordinarily inspired him, Balaam cries out: "Balac king of the Moabites hath brought me from Aram, from the mountains of the east: Come, said he, and curse Jacob: make haste and detest Israel. How shall I curse him, whom God hath not cursed?" (Numbers 23:7) Today there is another people blessed by God. Woe to him who curses them! From the Neros and the Julians, to the Voltaires and the old or more recent Robespierres, there is no shortage of examples of those who made the attempt.

Balaam declares: "This people shall dwell alone, and shall not be reckoned among the nations." (Numbers 23:9)

Also alone like Israel, the Church separates itself and distinguishes itself from any other society by its faith and by its law. It is a separate people that does not count itself among nations. Other nations can be vanquished; but the Church, who can triumph over it?

Furious to hear a blessing on Israel when he commands cursing, Balac leads Balaam to another hill to change his mind. But the soothsayer continues in these terms: "God is not a man, that he should lie, nor as the son of man, that he should be changed. Hath he said then, and will he not do? Hath he spoken, and will he not fulfil?" (Numbers 23:19) This is a troubling message for the high and mighty politicians of this world.

Balaam continues: "There is no idol in Jacob, neither is there an image god to be seen in Israel." (Numbers 23:21)

In the world, each has their idol. This person worships money, that one worships the flesh, while another adores public opinion, the spirit, the ideas of the age. In the Church everyone worships only the Lord God, Who is even more present before His new people than He was with the old.

The blessing continues on Israel: "The Lord his God is with him, and the sound of the victory of the king in him." (Numbers 23:21) Who can recount the victories that the Church won through Jesus Christ its King, and that Jesus Christ won through His Church?

"God hath brought him out of Egypt, whose strength is like to the rhinoceros." (Numbers 23:22)

Twenty times God delivered His Church from the hand of the Pharaohs. The rhinoceros is patient and strong; slow to anger, but terrible in his anger. Then, with a blow of his single horn, he pierces the elephant, this is a symbol of wisdom and power. Wise and mighty of the earth, let not Divine patience be an encouragement to you to continue in sin; and you, just and faithful ones waiting for justice, let not the Divine slowness in rising to just anger be a scandal to you. God is patient, but He is strong, and His anger grows all the more formidable in accordance with the measure of His patience and slowness to strike.

"Behold the people shall rise up as a lioness, and shall lift itself up as a lion." (Numbers 23:24)

Ah! Do not oppose the march of Israel; the people needs be arrive at the land which was promised to them. Do not oppose the march of the Church: it needs be that it reach the ends of the globe and last until the end of the ages. All nations, all ages are promised to it; the earth and the ages were given to it. Woe to him who dares to provoke the Lion of Judah! From the Robespierres to the Neros, and from the Voltaires to Juliens, there is no shortage of examples in history.

King Balac becomes angry, he leads Balaam to another hill. But, at the sight of the beautiful order that reigns in the camp of Israel, the soothsayer is ecstatic, and quite besides himself, exclaims: "How beautiful are your pavilions, O Jacob; How beautiful are your tents, O Israel!" (Numbers 24: 5)

Obviously from the top of his hill Balaam prophetically saw figured in the camp of Israel the future Church, which always on the move, always at war, lives under a tent so to speak because it does not hold fast to the earth and as it is only passing through.

"Lying down he hath slept as a lion, and as a lioness, whom none shall dare to rouse. He that blesseth thee, shall also himself be blessed: he that curseth thee shall be reckoned accursed." (Numbers 24:9)

The Star of Jacob

History attests that since the establishment of the Church there is not a prince, not a people that has become great unless he or they have devoted and consecrated themselves to the service and defence of the new people of God.   It is enough to name the Pelagiuses, the Charles Martels, the Pépins, the Charlemagnes, the Godefroys, the St. Louis, the Hunyadis, the Scanderbergs, the Don Juans, the Sobieskis, heroes forever blessed because they stood up for the freedom of the Church of Jesus Christ. It is enough to recall Spain and France, so magnanimous, so generous, so strong and so great while one was governed by the 'Most Catholic King', the other by the 'Most Christian King'.

In his frustration, King Balac claps his hands together, but in vain. Balaam resumes and cries: "I shall see him, but not now: I shall behold him, but not near. A star shall rise out of Jacob and a sceptre shall spring up from Israel: and shall strike the chiefs of Moab, and shall waste all the children of Seth," (Numbers 24:17) that is to say all men, who all are the sons of Seth of Noah.

The three wise men saw it, this marvellous star and they came to worship the King. This King, Who, coming out of Israel, is the only One Whose sceptre extends by right on all the sons of Seth and of Noah until the very end of time. Woe to anyone who resists: for him, that sceptre will turn into a rod and it will be broken upon him.

A Prophet Like Moses

Moses prepares for death. Israel crowds around the great man; they do not want to lose a single one of his last words. There is nothing so solemn like the supreme farewell of the majestic old man. In a voice that the years have only made more imposing, he recalls the miracles which attested to both the divine nature of his mission and the all-powerful goodness of the God of Jacob. He repeats and explains once again the law of Sinai. He announces his own death, and, piercing the shadows of the future with his prophetic gaze, he unfolds in advance the whole history of Israel; its coming infidelity and its ingratitude, the chastisements which will be the result, the dispersion of the nation, its repentance and the restoration. These facts have come to pass. Blessed by heaven as long as it remained faithful to the law of Moses, punished each time it forgot it, Israel was finally dispersed by Nebuchadnezzar, then restored by Cyrus. The fulfilment of these last predictions of the august old man confirms the inspiration which animated him, when, in these same farewells, in a voice more solemn than ever, he added this prophetic announcement: "The Lord thy God will raise up to thee a prophet of thy nation and of thy brethren like unto me: him thou shalt hear," - *'Prophetam de gente tua et de fratribus tuis, sicut me, rouscitabit tibi Dominus Deus tuus: ipsum audies.'* (Deut 18:15)

After Moses, how many prophets arose in the midst of Israel! But not one has equalled Moses: not one has been, like Moses, prophet, miracle-worker,

saviour, founder, legislator, king in fact and more than king, without being so in name, and all of these at the same time. Not Joshua, who was just a wonder-worker and saviour, nor Samuel who was only a prophet, wonder-worker and judge. Not David, who was only a warrior, prophet and king, nor Elias, who was just a prophet and wonder-worker. Not even the sublime Isaiah, nor the majestic Daniel come close to the great Moses. None of them, moreover, presented themselves as the great prophet announced by the august dying man. Jesus alone declares that He is this extraordinary envoy foretold by Moses.

The Jews refused to recognize this. "It is Moses himself who accuses you," Jesus said to them, "Moses in whom you trust. If you had faith in Moses, perhaps you would also believe in me, for he wrote of me." (John 5: 45-46)

In fact, only Jesus brings together in His Person all the traits of the liberator of Israel, and at the same time He surpasses him on each point.

Prophet like Moses and more than Moses. He not only discloses the future; He reveals the depths of hearts, He reveals the most intimate secrets of the Divinity.

Wonder-worker like Moses, and more than Moses. It is not through vengeful scourges and plagues, and it is not only on the material world that His power is exercised. He applies it directly to men, His power is only shown through benefits. Jesus does not strike the sinner, He heals. He does not kill, He resurrects; and if sometimes He is severe and terrible, it is only toward the infernal spirits that He expels from the bodies of the possessed.

Saviour like Moses, and more than Moses. Moses only saved one people, and in the process lost another. Jesus, however, saves all people: only those who refuse to be saved are lost.

Founder like Moses, and more than Moses. Moses founded for a specific time, Moses founded only the earth. Jesus founded for all time, and what He founded will last until the end of the ages: "Behold I am with you all days, even to the consummation of the world" - *'Ecce ego vobiscum sum usque ad consummationem saeculi,'* (Matt. 28:20). His kingdom will continue for eternity: "And of his kingdom there shall be no end," - *'et regni ejus non erit finis.'* (Luke 1:33) Jesus founded in heaven; His kingdom is that of the heavens: "The kingdom of heaven is at hand," - *'appropinquavit regnum caelorum'*, (Matt. 10:7) and His kingdom is in this world and is exercised on this world, which He includes in His sphere of rule and which He rules over with all His highness; He does not come from this world, but from on high; "My kingdom is not of this world," - *'regnum meum non est de hoc mundo'*. (John 18:36)

Law-giver like Moses, and more than Moses. The law of Moses is engraved on stone, the law of Jesus is written in hearts. The law of Moses enlightens the intellect, but without strengthening the will. The law of Jesus is both light for the understanding and grace for the will: it declares what must be done, and gives the strength to do it. The law of Moses tolerates imperfection, the law of Jesus demands perfection. "Be you therefore perfect, as also your heavenly Father is perfect." (Matt. 5:48).

The law of Moses suffers certain exceptions which deviate from the ideal of the Divine commandments, while the law of Jesus adds counsels to the commandments that further strengthen and elevate them. Moses bases the law on hope and fear, on promises of reward and on threats of punishment, on the temporal goods and on the evils of the earth and of the times. Jesus promises nothing on earth and for the times anything other than suffering and the reproaches of the cross. He does not threaten famine, pestilence, or war, but, seemingly neglecting both the temporal goods and the temporal evils of earth, His gaze directs up to heaven while His finger points to hell. Hell — there is eternal misfortune. Heaven — there is eternal happiness.

Meanwhile, here below on earth, you have nothing to hope for, but you have nothing to fear; that is, nothing to hope for here as the temporal goods here below will pass, but you have nothing to fear as the evils here too will pass. However, beyond this globe, beyond this temporal time, both of which carry you away in their rapid course, you have everything to hope for, and you have everything to fear: everything to hope for in the justice and the goodness of Jesus if you are faithful to Him, while you have everything to fear from His justice and His wrath if you are unfaithful to Him. For if He leaves to your free will something of this temporal earth and of time, He nevertheless retains the high domain; He is and remains the Universal and Eternal Sovereign. For man is given a portion of time, a few days, a few years; to Jesus belongs all time, all days, all centuries, and beyond that, eternity: "Jesus Christ, yesterday, and today; and the same for ever," - *'Jesus Christus heri et hodie: ipse et in saecula'*. (Hebrews 13:8)

King by Divine Right

"Why have the Gentiles raged, and the people devised vain things? The kings of the earth stood up, and the princes met together, against the Lord and against his Christ." (Psalm 2:1) It seems that only a little longer, and it will be all over for His kingdom, that is to say, His Church. But, at the sight of these great futile outbursts, the Most High was content to smile at their proceedings: "He that dwelleth in heaven shall laugh at them: and the Lord shall deride them." (Psalm 2:2) In response, for His one and only answer, Christ limits Himself to calmly repeating that He is king: "I am appointed king by him over Sion his holy mountain, preaching his commandment," - *'Ego autem constitutus sum rex ab eo super Sion, montem sanctum ejus, praedicans praeceptum ejus.'* (Psalms 2:6)

Now open the Gospel. All their anger is indeed united against Jesus. The princes and people of Judah bring Him before Pilate, and accuse Him of having presented Himself as the King: 'We have found this man ... saying that he is Christ the king. *'Dicentem se Christum Regem esse'* (Luke 23:2) "Yes," Jesus replies: " I am king." - *'Quia Rex sum ego.'* (John 18:37) And in this quiet confirmation from Him, what is most frightening for those kings and people who would dare challenge Him for royalty is that His kingdom is not of this world, that the sceptre does not come from men, nor from Caesar, nor from the people, but from God and from God alone: "I am appointed King by him," - *'Ego autem constitutus sum Rex ab eo.'*

(Psalm 2:6) Shake with fury O kings, unite together against Him: but what can human force do against Divine Right?

Even if He were like you, only a simple mortal who today is proudly seated on a throne and tomorrow will be lying in the mire, you would be allowed to hope and wait for your turn for power. But, if Jesus reigns by Divine Right, He does not only exist as David and his house once did, that is, by virtue of a special and temporary mission – He reigns because He is the Son of God, God like His Father. Also, to the frustrated shaking of angry princes and nations that refuse to recognize His right and refuse to submit to His royalty, He only offers this response: "The Lord said to me, 'You are my Son; it is I who have begotten you this day." (Psalm 2:7)

Recognize Him, to Whom, on the day of His baptism in the Jordan and on the day of His Transfiguration, the same Voice says; "Thou art my beloved Son; in thee I am well pleased." (Luke 3:22) and "This is my beloved Son; hear him." (Luke 9:35)

Do not try to escape His empire; do not say that His Kingdom is neither 'in' this world nor 'on' this world. If His royalty is not 'of' this world, since it is comes from on high as mentioned, it nevertheless does not fail to extend itself 'on' this world, and to exercise itself 'in' this world. Do you not hear that God the Father has made Him Sovereign Master? After having established Him King and having declared Him to be His Son in the Psalm, He then addresses to Him these words: "Ask of me, and I will give thee the Gentiles for thy inheritance, and the utmost parts of the earth for thy possession," - *'et dabo tibi gentes haerediratem tuam et possessionem tuam terminos terrae.'* (Psalm 2:8) Is that not clear enough? Also hear Him in turn repeat to His apostles when He sends them in His Name to take possession of the kingdom which He conquered with His Blood: "All power has been given to me in heaven and on earth; go therefore, teach all nations. (Matt. 28:18-19) "You will be my witnesses ... to the ends of the earth." (Acts 1:8)

Take heed, O you who would dare to put limits to His power. For you, His sceptre would become the rod, for God said to Him: "You will rule them with a rod of iron, and you will break them like the potter's vessel:" - *'Reges eos in virga ferrea, et tanquam vas figuli confringes eos.'* (Psalm 2:9) The Psalmist then warns: "And now, O ye kings, understand: receive instruction, you that judge the earth. Serve ye the Lord with fear: and rejoice unto him with trembling. Embrace discipline, lest at any time the Lord be angry, and you perish from the just way." (Psalm 2:10)

Submit to Him: otherwise this prophecy will become historical truth for you as for with so many others.

The Sacrifice

"O God my God, look upon me: why hast thou forsaken me?" (Psalm 21:2) Who utters this desolate cry to the heavens? David fleeing from a rebellious son, or Jesus Christ nailed to the cross by an ungrateful and cruel people, or, the Church crucified in the person of its persecuted leader, whether this leader is a

Gregory VII, a Boniface VIII, a Pius VI, a Pius VII , or a Pius IX, or even the Eldest Daughter of the Church, the most Christian France of Clovis, of Charlemagne and of St. Louis? If Jesus from the top of His cross was able to repeat this complaint from the Psalm with even more truth than David, "My God, my God, why hast thou forsaken me," (Matt. 27:46), is it not permissible to think that, in the life of the Church and of the Catholic nations, they find themselves having the right to complain like the Master?

"In thee have our fathers hoped: they have hoped, and thou hast delivered them. They cried to thee, and they were saved: they trusted in thee, and were not confounded. But I am a worm, and no man: the reproach of men, and the outcast of the people." (Psalm 21: 5-7) See Jesus beaten, mocked, scourged, crowned with thorns, dragged through the streets, succumbing under the burden of the cross, nailed to this infamous wood — is He not become as the earthworm that the passer-by crushes with contempt? "But I am a worm." Hear the cries of the princes and elders of the people, which are instantly repeated with a tremendous clamour by the maddened populace : "Not this man, but Barabbas," - *'Non hunc, sed Barabbam'* (John 18:40). No, not this one, but deliver to us the bandit, the seditious rebel, the murderer, Barabbas! "What shall I do then with Jesus that is called Christ?" (Matt. 27:22) — To death! To death! To the cross: "Away with him; away with him; crucify him," - *'Tolle, tolle, crucifige um'*. (John 19:15) He has indeed become the opprobrium of men and the revulsion of the populace. But is this not also the history of the Church? And how many times has Barabbas been preferred to over Jesus, present and living in the person of His Vicar and his priests? Well then! You got your Barabbas! Jerusalem, are you now pleased with yourself?

"All they that saw me have laughed me to scorn: they have spoken with the lips, and wagged the head. He hoped in the Lord, let him deliver him: let him save him, seeing he delighteth in him." (Psalm 21:8-9) You have heard the psalm, now open the Gospel: "And they that passed by, blasphemed him, wagging their heads, and saying ... He trusted in God; let him now deliver him if he will have him." (Matt. 27, 39-40, 43) Follow Jesus Christ now suffering in His Church, you will hear the same challenges, the same taunts repeated.

"There is none to help me," - *'Quoniam non est qui adjuvet.'* (Psalm 21:12) And where are they, the helpers and defenders of Jesus Christ Who again is nailed to suffering and humiliation, reduced to the immobility of helplessness in the person of the head and the main members of the Church, which is His mystical Body?

From His Church, as from the top of His cross, He can say with more truth than David:

"They surrounded me," (Psalm 21:30) – (Pius IX a prisoner in the Vatican);

"They have opened their mouths against me, as a lion ravening and roaring," (v. 14) - (a figure of the liberal press and the impious tribune).

"I have been poured out like water," (v. 15) - (by the shedding of all My Blood), "and all my bones have been scattered" (v. 15)– ('my bones', a figure of all that sustained Me, all that was My material strength. Where are the kings, the warriors, the Christian

peoples that were formerly supporters and defenders of the Church, of the Pope, of Jesus Christ?)

"My heart is become like wax melting in the midst of my bowels ... my tongue hath cleaved to my jaws ... many dogs have encompassed me: the council of the malignant hath besieged me." (vs. 15-17) - (The dog here represents what is most vile in the wicked and ignorant populace that allows itself to be so easily incited by the most cruel and senseless outcries.)

The freedom of speech prepares and engenders the license of action — the dog barks; then if you do not silence him, he become ferocious, he bites and tears. Listen to the following:

"For many dogs have encompassed me ... they have dug my hands and feet. They have numbered all my bones. And they have looked and stared upon me." (Psalm 21: 17-18) Torn asunder by flogging, Jesus let all His bones be seen, and even down to the depths of His bowels. However, instead of sympathizing with His pain, the barbarians take pleasure in staring at Him and with their gaze they probe the interior of His half-opened flanks: "And they have looked and stared upon me."- *'ipsi vero consideraverunt me et inspexerunt me.'* Next, "they parted my garments amongst them; and upon my vesture they cast lots." (Psalm 21: 19) Is it David the psalmist who speaks, or rather is it not St. John, eyewitness of what the prophetic king saw a thousand years in advance? The Evangelist says: "The soldiers, therefore, when they had crucified him, took his garments, (and they made four parts, to every soldier a part,) and also his coat. Now the coat was without seam, woven from the top throughout. They said then one to another: Let us not cut it, but let us cast lots for it, whose it shall be ." (John 19, 23-24)

Here we see Calvary, the Psalm shows Him defeated, stripped ... but by a sudden setback, the scene changes: the same sorrowful Psalm now shows the universe prostrate itself at the feet of the Crucified One, adoring Him as God, recognizing Him as the King: "For the kingdom is the Lord's; and he shall have dominion over the nations," - *'Quoniam Domini est regnum, et ipse dominabitur gentium'*. (Psalm 21:29) Indeed, such is the denouement of the terrible drama of Calvary, and, each time the Passion of the Leader is renewed in His Mystical Body of the Church or in some of its members, this will always be the triumphant outcome: "For the kingdom is the Lord's; and he shall have dominion over the nations," - *'Quoniam Domini est regnum: et ipse dominabitur gentium.'*

He will reign; but the crown will come at the price of sacrifice. David announces it and St. Paul repeats it. When He entered this world, the Infant God said in His Heart: "Sacrifice and oblation (of the old law) thou didst not desire;" (Psalm 39:7) "Sacrifice and oblation thou wouldest not: but a body thou hast fitted to me, Holocausts for sin did not please thee." (Hebrews 10:5-6) "Then said I, Behold I come. In the head of the book it is written of me that I should do thy will: O my God, I have desired it, and thy law in the midst of my heart." (Psalm 39:8-9)

He obeyed. He sacrificed Himself. He will therefore be the King of nations. "Thou wilt make me head of the Gentiles." - *'Constitues me in caput gentium.'* (Psalm. 17, 44). His reign will last as long as the sun; "And he shall continue with the sun," - *'et permanebut cum sole'*. (Psalm 71:5), "And he shall rule from sea to sea, and from the river unto the ends of the earth." (Psalm 71:8). Recognize by these features the

One Who declares to His envoys that He is with them until the consummation of the ages: "Behold I am with you all days, even to the consummation of the world,"- *'Ecce ego vobiscum sum usque ad consummationem saeculi,'* (Matt. 28-20), and Who orders them to attest to His power to the ends of the globe; "You shall be witnesses unto me ... even to the uttermost part of the earth,"- *'eritis mihi testes ... usque ad ultimum terrae.'* (Acts 1:8) Also, "all kings of the earth shall adore him: all nations shall serve him," - *'et adorabunt eum omnes reges terrae; omnes gentes servint ei,'* (Psalm 71:11). "The earth is the Lord's and the fulness thereof: the world, and all they that dwell therein," - *'Domini est terra et plenitudo ejus; orbis terrarum et universi qui inhabitant in eo'.* (Psalm 23:). We cannot emphasize this point too much, we cannot repeat too much that if Jesus Christ is the Eternal King of Heaven, He is also the King of temporal matter; that if He is the King of souls, He is also the King of bodies; that if He is the King of men, He is also the King of nations.

But if He is the King of nations, of bodies, of the ages of the earth, it is so that He may lead men to the Eternal Kingdom of Heaven. The prophet foresaw in advance what the apostles witnessed with their own eyes; he glimpsed the victory and triumph that comes after the battle. "Lift up your gates," the prophet cries, "lift up your gates, O ye princes, and be ye lifted up, O eternal gates: and the King of Glory shall enter in. Who is this King of glory," the celestial princes asked? "The Lord who is strong and mighty: the Lord mighty in battle." - *'Dominus potens in praelio'.* (Psalm 23:7-9) Why then are you afraid of the great day of battle, O timid Christians? What do you have to fear? He is the strong and powerful King. Combat is necessary to bring forth one's power and strength — to refuse the fight would be to refuse the triumph. If in the past Christ had to suffer to enter into His glory, if He had to ascend to Calvary before ascending to Heaven, then today as back then, He must suffer and fight in the person of the Pope, who is His Vicar, and He must suffer and fight in the Church, which is His Body, so that both the Pope and the Church can be associated with His triumph and glory.

<u>The Triumph</u>

"The Lord said to my Lord: Sit thou at my right hand."- *'Dixit Dominus Domino meo: Sede a dextris meis.'* (Psalm 109:1) One day Jesus asked the Pharisees: "What think you of Christ? Whose son is he?" - "Of David," replied the doctors. Jesus replied, "How then doth David in spirit call him Lord, saying: The Lord said to my Lord, Sit on my right hand, until I make thy enemies thy footstool? If David then call him Lord, how is he his son?" (Matt. 22:42-45) The Pharisees did not respond. They knew that Jesus was the son of David. It would have been necessary to then confess that He was also the Lord of David, that is to say the Christ, that is to say — *God.* His miracles, moreover, said it quite loudly. The Pharisees of that time did what the Pharisees of all times do - they remained silent - and doubtless fearing that they would be forced to recognize the truth, they no longer dared to question Him.

But as for us, we listen to the speech that the Lord addresses to the Lord. "Sit thou at my right hand," - *'Sede a dextris meis.'* Sit down: that is, in the quiet and assured possession of the throne and the empire. "At my right hand", to my right: the place of honour next to the one who speaks; but the One Who speaks here is the Sovereign, "Lord" - *'Dominus'*, it is God Himself.

"Sit thou at my right hand: Until I make thy enemies thy footstool."

Let us recognize here the One of Whom Saint Paul said: "For he must reign, until he hath put all his enemies under his feet." (1. Cor. 15:25) How many footstools have there been – all the Caiaphas, the Pilates, the Neros, the Juliens!

This is because He holds the sceptre, the rod of Divine power. "The Lord will send forth the sceptre of thy power out of Sion," - *'Virgam virtutis tuae emittet Dominus ex Sion.'* (Psalm 109:2) Was it not, in fact, from Sion that Jesus extended His sceptre over the world?

But here is the characteristic feature of the dominion of Jesus Christ. "Rule thou in the midst of thy enemies." - *'Dominare in medio inimicorum tuorum.'* (Psalm 109:2) Dominate, be the Master, even in the midst of Thy enemies. Let us open the Gospel. Notice His dominating power bursts forth always at the moment when His enemies around Him believe they are sure of seizing and vanquishing Him.

The doctors banded together to catch Him out in His words. But He speaks with so much authority: "teaching them as one having power", *'potestatem habens'*, (Matt. 7:29) that the people exclaim: "Never has a man spoken like this man." (John 7:46) "Rule thou in the midst of thy enemies." - *'Dominare in medio inimicorum'*. [48]

At the Garden of Olives, the soldiers advance to seize Him; but a few words will be enough for Him to show that He is the Master. "I am he" -*'Ego sum'* -He said, and suddenly the soldiers roll before His feet. "As soon therefore as he had said to them: I am he; they went backward, and fell to the ground." (John 18:6) "Rule thou in the midst of thy enemies."- *'Dominare in medio inimicorum.'*

Follow Him before Pilate. They flogged Him, jeered at Him, beat Him. On His head I see a crown of thorns, on His shoulders a shred of purple, in His hand a paltry reed. The princes and priests of the nation surround Him and overwhelm Him with their false accusations: with loud cries an entire people demands for His death, and that His death be on the cross. And it is then that He calmly declares that He is the King: "That I am a king" - *'Quia Rex sum ego.'* (John 18:37) "Rule thou in the midst of thy enemies."- *'Dominare in medio inimicorum.'*

See Him on the cross. His triumphant enemies pass before Him, challenging and insulting Him. But the sun disappears, the earth trembles, the rocks split, the veil of the temple is torn, the tombs are opened and

---

48   The ministers also attempted to lay hands on Him, but then dared not do so: "*The rulers and Pharisees sent ministers to apprehend him. ... And some of them would have apprehended him: but no man laid hands on him. The ministers therefore came to the chief priests and the Pharisees. And they said to them: Why have you not brought him? The ministers answered: Never did man speak like this man.*" (John 7:39, 44-46)

the dead are resurrected, sinners are converted, and the people withdraw, repeating with the Roman centurion: "Truly this man was righteous, truly He was the Son of God." - "Rule thou in the midst of thy enemies."- *'Dominare in medio inimicorum.'*

The pontiffs of the synagogue and the deicidal princes have affixed their seals to His tomb; around His tomb they ranged their soldiers. Vain precautions. From the bosom of death, and from the midst of His enemies, Jesus rises triumphant. - "Rule thou in the midst of thy enemies."- *'Dominare in medio inimicorum.'*

By this trait we also recognize His work. Browse the annals of the Church. Never does its power appear more brilliantly than in these solemn and terrible moments when people and kings seem to have given themselves the order to enslave or overthrow it. Let us only recall Leo the Great in the midst of barbarism, St. Gregory VII enveloped by the ferocious hordes of the Germanic tyrant, Pius VII at Fontainebleau, and see Pius IX at the Vatican, more master and more sovereign than the crowned slaves who hold him there or who leave him captive there.   "Rule thou in the midst of thy enemies."- *'Dominare in medio inimicorum.'*

So He must dominate and rule, and why? Listen. "With thee is the principality in the day of thy strength: in the brightness of the saints: from the womb before the day star I begot thee," - *'Tecum principium, in die virtutis tuae, in splendoribus sanctorum: ex utero ante luciferum genui te.'* (Psalm 109:3)   Literally, according to the Hebrew: "I willed you, I animated you in the day of your strength, in the splendours of holiness. From my womb, before the dawn, you were begotten." The One to Whom this language is addressed therefore exists before dawn, that is, before all Creation. Begotten from the very 'womb' of God Who is absolutely indivisible, begotten, not created, He is God like the One Who begets Him. And this explains why His domination is assured.

"The Lord hath sworn, and he will not repent: Thou art a priest for ever according to the order of Melchisedech." (Psalm 109:4) God repented of having created the pure spirits, the angels; God repented of having united spirit and flesh to compose man.[49] In other words, God, Who, in His immutable will, loves good and hates evil wherever He finds it, God loves the angel and man as long as they remain good and he 'hates'[50] them as soon as they become evil. But he will

---

49 God repented having made man when the earth grew corrupted to where He was compelled to send the Flood to cleanse the earth. *"And God seeing that the wickedness of men was great on the earth, and that all the thought of their heart was bent upon evil at all times, it repented him that he had made man on the earth. And being touched inwardly with sorrow of heart, He said: I will destroy man, whom I have created, from the face of the earth, from man even to beasts, from the creeping thing even to the fowls of the air, for it repenteth me that I have made them."* (Gen. 6:5-6) The Douay-Rheims explains the terms 'repented' and 'sorrow' are used to declare the enormity of the sins of men, which was so provoking as to cause their Creator to destroy them, creatures whom before He had so much favoured. If God felt this way about the universal corruption of mankind, Fr de Boylesve must have assumed God also felt the same way when Lucifer and the rebel angels fell, for in the book of Job we find the following passage: *"Shall man be justified in comparison of God, or shall a man be more pure than his maker? Behold they that serve him are not steadfast, and in his angels he found wickedness."* (Job 4:17-18)

50 That is, there is a 'holy hatred', a complete detestation for evil and sin, just as there is a 'holy jealousy', for God

not repent of this Eternal Priesthood which results from the union of the Word with human nature through the Incarnation.

The great design of God the Creator is realized in the Person of the Mediator God, that is, in Jesus Christ, Mediator between God and mankind. Through Jesus Christ the world of bodies and the world of spirits, both summed up in man, are united with God forever: "Thou art a priest for ever," - '*Tu es sacerdos in aeternum*'.

Therefore, woe to man, woe to the nation that opposes the reign of Jesus. "The Lord at thy right hand hath broken kings in the day of his wrath. He shall judge among nations, he shall fill ruins: he shall crush the heads in the land of the many." (Psalm 109:5-6) Look and see: what are these ruins He fills and piles up on all sides? It is what remains of those empires, of these dynasties that try to oppose the reign that Jesus Christ claims and exercises here below through the Church and through the Pope: "he shall fill ruins"- '*implebit ruinas.*' Where are those high-heads who only just yesterday stood up and agitated themselves threateningly against the Vicar of Jesus Christ? All of a sudden they they collided with a crash, they shattered against each other: "He shall crush the heads in the land of the many." - '*Conquassabit capita in terra multorum*'. The triumph, it is true, is not obtained without combat.   Jesus therefore drinks from the torrent of tribulation, for the Psalm concludes with:

---

declares He is a jealous God that will not abide another god before Him – we are His creation and He is justly entitled to all our love and worship as a husband may expect from his bride. Notice again that abandoning the laws of God and worshipping false gods and idols in the Old Testament is equated with 'adultery' and 'fornication' against God.

"He shall drink of the torrent in the way," - *'De torrente in via bibet'*. (Psalm 109:7) But He only drinks there in passing, "in the way" - *'in via'*. All the evils came together to overwhelm Him. "He humbled himself," says St. Paul, "becoming obedient unto death, even to the death of the cross. For which cause God also hath exalted him, and hath given him a name which is above all names: that in the name of Jesus every knee should bow, of those that are in heaven, on earth, and under the earth: And that every tongue should confess that the Lord Jesus Christ is in the glory of God the Father." (Philippians 2:7-11) These lines of the Apostle, what are they if not the expanded translation of this line of the prophet in the psalm: "He shall drink of the torrent in the way," therefore for this very reason, "he shall lift up the head." - *'De torrente in via bibet, propterea exaltabit caput.'*

And these words are still the continuing history of the Church. In its journey through the centuries, the Church encounters the torrent of persecution; she drinks from it as she passes, then she gets up again more pure and freer than before.

Everything that opposes its progress is shoved aside, or overturns and breaks. Ruins are the only monuments which remind future ages of the vain attempts made by the pride of the impious. And the Church advances its dominion through its leader who is the Pope, in all grandeur, all power, all royalty. "He shall drink of the torrent in the way: therefore shall he lift up the head." - *'De torrente in via bibet, propterea exaltabit caput'*.

The Hebrews and the Greeks

The history of Jesus Christ is also that of the secular world, even before His advent on earth. Just as there is no true greatness to be found after His coming except with those men and nations that dedicate themselves to the cause of His reign, in the same way, all those who left their mark on the movement of human progress before His birth owe their glory to the assistance they brought to the preparation of His empire over souls without realising they were doing so.

Let us first consider the founders of the most illustrious cities of Greece and the first civilizers of this small country which, in turn, must civilize the world. They appear at the same time as the holy patriarchs who were the fathers of the people of God.

Shortly after Abraham, Inachus founded Argos. Between the time of Joseph and Moses, Cecrops founded Athens, and Casmus founded Thebes. After Joshua, Pelopes dominated the peninsula, which will be called,the Peloponnese. It was therefore from Egypt and Phoenicia that the Greeks received civilization. Cecrops was Egyptian, Inachus and Cadmus were Phoenicians, Pelops was Phrygian. Thus the Canaan race still found itself at the head of the civilizing movement in the region. But the impulse to do so actually comes from on high. When Inachus left the land of Canaan, Abraham appeared there. How could his example remain without influence on peoples who professed the highest veneration for his virtue? The moral culture of the Egyptians is praised; but, their civilization could not have remained a stranger to

Jacob, who saved this people and who governed them through his son Joseph. Cecrops parted from Egypt after the time of Joseph. Thus Providence presided with special attention over the primary education of His little people who will play such a great role in the history of the world, and we see from the beginning there have been real relationships between the Greeks and the Hebrews.

It is true that today certain men, who only value the power of numbers and the masses, have difficulty restraining an amused smile when we speak to them about the importance of this corner of the earth that was Greece in those days. True, we know Athens did not equal even a suburb of Paris, but we also know that neither genius, nor strength, nor greatness, depends on number, size or extent. China is ten times larger than France today, and there are ten times more Chinese than French people. If it comes to influence, will you dare to compare the two peoples?[51] Greece was a small country, and the Greeks when taken all together were only a small people: however, after the Hebrews, and with the Romans, they hold the first rank in the ancient western world.

As if the people of Israel were already still too numerous, out of twelve tribes God reserves just two to give the Saviour and freedom to the world: Judah and Benjamin. Likewise, among the small tribes of Greece, two stand out and dominate: Sparta and Athens. Militaristic Sparta was rough and robust like the tribe of Benjamin, which the Scriptures compared to the

---

51   Despite its size and population, China was considered backward and underdeveloped when compared to France and Europe the time Fr de Boylesve wrote this.

ferocious and ravishing wolf.[52] Athens was the centre and beacon of Greek society, just as the tribe of Judah was in Israel.

If we recall the kinship which united the Spartans and the Jews (1 Machabees 12, 21),[53] we can perhaps better explain the liberating mission and the works of that Hercules, whose descendants under the name of the Heraclides constituted the elite of the Spartan people.[54]

Now, it is said the ancestors of Alexander the Great are those heroes that became figures in their myths. Alexander, just like Cyrus, was led by the hand of God, and without knowing it, was destined to prepare the ways to Christian unity.

The parallelism continues for a long time between the two peoples for the liberating heroes appear there at the same time. While Israel has its Aods, its Baracs, its Gideons, its Jephthahs, the Greeks have Hercules, Theseus, Jason, while Samson of the Old Testament is a contemporary of Achilles.

---

52   "Benjamin a ravenous wolf, in the morning shall eat the prey, and in the evening shall divide the spoil." (Gen. 49:27)

53   This passage in 1 Machabees (21) reveals the blood relation between the Jews and the Spartans: "It is found in writing concerning the Spartans, and the Jews, that they are brethren, and that they are of the stock of Abraham."

54   According to Greek myth, the Heraclides, or Heraklides, were the numerous descendants in patrilineal lineage of Hercules. A number of Heraclids include Macaria, Lamus, Manto, Bianor, Tlepolemus, and Telephus, a group of Dorian kings who according to literary tradition in Greek mythology, claimed a right to rule through Hercules and conquered the Peloponnesian kingdoms of Mycenae, Sparta , and Argos.

<u>Royalty</u>

In the same year, 1095 before Jesus Christ (BC), in a singular contrast, Athens was victorious thanks to the devotion of its king Codrus who then abolished royalty; while, peaceful and happy under the paternal judiciary care of Samuel, the people of God decide to demand a king.

It has been said that for Athens the abolition of kings was a sign of its greatness. But, they have forgotten that from the time of Codrus to Solon, five centuries pass, and these five centuries pass by without any recorded history, and consequently, without any glory for Athens. Could we not conclude that the abolition of royalty served rather to *delay* the developmental progress of that fickle and frivolous city? Besides, history displays that the Athenians were only great when they were led by a single man and by a superior man. They only need to name Miltiades, Themistocles, Cimon, Pericles. And let us not forget that democracy, a system that engenders jealously, suspicions, fickleness, capriciousness, far from supporting these great men, only hindered them, when it did not outright overthrow them. Above all, let us recall that despite his zeal for freedom and his aversion to royalty, Demosthenes never ceased to repeat that the successes of Philip and, consequently, the enslavement of Athens, have their cause in the very nature of democracy. But let us leave Athens, and seek in the first people of God the ideal of the reign of Jesus Christ, and, at the same time, the pattern of the most perfect government.

Forgetting that Jesus Christ is King and that He is *par excellence* the King, the enemies of royalty do not fail to point out that God Himself inflicted a severe reprimand on the children of Israel when they took the liberty of asking for kings. But it must be observed that this Divine reprimand does not fall on the monarchical form itself, since, from Moses to Samuel inclusive, that is to say since it was a nation, Israel has only been happy and peaceful in times when it was delivered, defended and governed by one man. What offended God was Israel's request to be governed by kings like the *other nations of the earth*, and thus would withdraw from the special action of His Providence directed on them.

"They have not rejected thee," the Lord said to His prophet, "but Me, that I should not reign over them." (1 Kings 8:7) However, after and despite this rebuke, God gives kings to Israel, and it will even be through kings such as David and Solomon that He will elevate this people to the pinnacle of glory and prosperity.

<u>Institutions and Mankind</u>

Great importance is attached to institutions and laws. Far from us is the thought of contesting this importance. Let us observe, however, that it is not institutions and laws that make a people happy, strong and great; it is the men of a nation. It is not institutions and laws that make men; it is men who make institutions and laws – that is, civil laws, the only ones we speaking about here. Let us further add that it is also men who observe and enforce institutions and laws.

Now, let us present certain scenarios. Let us suppose a civil law is good; but there is a man that is wicked and strong; such a man will break the law. Then, let us suppose a law is bad, but a man that is good and strong will break that evil law. Then, let us consider the men of a nation are good, but weak; a law that is wise and good would be in vain then, for the wicked will make fun of a law that cannot be maintained by force or power.

If there ever was a people that possessed wise institutions and laws, it was certainly the people of Israel instituted and formed by God Himself. And yet this people only remained wise and good, and was only happy when it was governed by a virtuous man and was firm enough to maintain the observation of the law.

Divine Intervention

There is nothing more blind than the libertine in his crude sensuality, and the businessman and man of money in his material positivism. Contemporary rationalism responds with a sneer to those who speak of Divine intervention acting in human matters; however, even the myths and history of the pagans agree with the Bible in this point of divine intervention.

Their mythology presents their heroes as envoys of the gods, and even as demi-gods, while their historical accounts present their great men in connection with the divinity that inspired them. Lycurgus relies on the oracle, Socrates has his familiar *daemon.*[55] These fictions contain the common sense response to the sneer of the so-called philosophers and so-called politicians of our times: they attest to the widespread sentiment among all men that deliverance and salvation can only come from God alone.

The saviours of Israel are also sent from God, but unlike the myths of the pagans, the Bible does not make them demi-gods. Nevertheless, what a difference between the heroes of the people of the true God and those of the pagan people! Strengthened by the very same strength of the One Who inspires them, these generous men rose up to save their brothers. Around them a whole people groans and trembles. They are an enslaved people who do not dare to shake off their chains. The Aods, the Deborahs, the Gideons, the Jephthahs, the Samons, the Davids present themselves. They see the impossible stand before them. What does it matter? It is God Who sends them. They advance in the Name of God, and in the Name of God they dare to do the impossible. Goliath is overthrown, Israel is saved, David will be king — and through this king the people of God reach their peak.

---

55   Lycurgus was the legendary lawgiver of Sparta. He is credited with establishing the military-oriented reformation of Spartan society in accordance with the Oracle of Apollo at Delphi. All his reforms promoted the three Spartan virtues: equality, military fitness, and austerity. With regards to the philosopher Socrates, a 'daemon' is not a demon – it is a guiding spirit that was considered a deity. One may possible find its closest comparison in having a guardian angel, although the Greeks considered their guiding spirits minor deities. Or, it may have been the voice of conscience mistaken as a deity. In Plato's '*Apology of Socrates,*' Socrates claimed to have a *daimōnion* (literally, a "divine something") in the form of a "voice" that warned him against making mistakes and errors, but never actually told him what to do.

EXVL
TENT
LÆTEN
TVR
EXVL
TENT
TVR

David

Trained in the harsh school of misfortune, David will be the great king, and, after Moses, the greatest man of Israel. His whole life was a struggle. While an adolescent, he was only an obscure shepherd; but from that point on he defeats the bears and the lions to save his flock. As a young man he overthrew Goliath and saved the people of God. His reward will be the jealousy of Saul. Pursued, hunted like a wild beast, we always see him with weapons in hand, first to defend his own life against an unjust persecutor, then to support his rights to the throne against those who refuse to recognize them, and, finally to definitively defeat the eternal enemies of the people of Israel.

Through the power of victories and conquests, he believes he has assured himself the right to rest. But woe to him for whom leisure becomes *idleness*! A moment of this fatal idleness was enough to overthrow the invincible warrior and the sublime prophet, and, thus in his old age will be desolated by the revolt of a son. But the royal penitent rises by his very abasement.

Then, no longer thinking of reposing, and knowing that princes have only received power to honour God, he devotes the treasures which he got through his victories to prepare for the construction of that famous temple which will be the figure of the Church, like David himself was the figure of Jesus Christ, and also the symbolic type of the Christian king.

There are two men in David: the prophet and the king, the man of God and the man of the country. This warrior holds two swords which he wields with equal honour: the sword of prayer and the sword of the soldier. By his sword he slays the visible enemies, by his prayers he exterminates the invisible enemies. With Solomon his son, he closes the gallery of these astonishing men who were called by their lives to represent the type of the hero, the great king *par excellence*. He opens the series of great prophecies which will announce the life and death, the battles, the triumphs and the reign of the Liberator promised to Adam, to Abraham, to Isaac, to Jacob, and solemnly predicted by the dying Moses.

The tabernacle of the desert is replaced by the temple. David, the warrior and conquering king who spent almost his entire life in a tent so to speak, is succeeded by the peaceful and orderly King Solomon, who, by erecting the temple of God, crowns the work of his father.

David: he represents Jesus Christ, obscure and unknown at first during the days of His hidden life, then fighting against the enemies of God during the days of His public life, finally pursued and abandoned on the day of His Passion, of which Absalom's revolt was only a figure.

Solomon, in the first part of his reign, represents Jesus Christ glorious and triumphant, Jesus Christ founding His Church and erecting in the world this unique temple to the One True God.

All the glories, all the arts of culture are summed up in Solomon, who will remain the most complete type of civilization taken in all its extent.

All the glories too, all the arts will gather around Jesus Christ, Who Alone is the Principle and the First Reason of all greatness and all wisdom.

Once Again - Civilization

Here is where we return to the subject regarding the race of Cain and Cham and the former concessions we made regarding their involvement in civilization. No, we will not allow the cursed, of whatever kind, to have a monopoly on civilization. The children of men, the sons of the time, were only the labourers and pioneers of the children of God. To the children of God, and to them alone, belongs the honour of all progress in the arts and sciences, the sum total of which constitutes true civilization.

We have seen that the arts were invented by the sons of Cain. Jubal created music; but this sublime art does not reach the ideal in its application, which is divine worship. And so it is a son of Seth, it is Enos who first begins to solemnly celebrate the name of the Lord, and it is with the inspired songs of David, that music becomes a divine harmony.

Construction of the Ark

Without disputing the importance of pastoral art, it is impossible not to recognize the superiority of the farmer over the simple shepherd. Cultivating the soil requires work that is both more energetic on the part of the body and more intellectual on the part of the mind; farming provides both man and the herds themselves with more complete resources for their substance and well-being. Noah, who began to cultivate the soil, was therefore more advanced in civilization, even in material terms, than this Jabel of the race of Cain, who was the father of shepherds.

This same Jabel builds tents, and Tubalcain, his brother, shapes iron and bronze to his liking. But what are Jabel's tents compared to the ark of Noah, an admirable construction that requires all of Tubalcain's metallurgical resources! The ark, moreover, is the first ship to appear in history. And of all the arts, the boldest and most sociable is that of the navigator, which unites peoples whom the oceans seemed to have separated forever. God, Who Himself ordered and directed the construction of the first ship, cursed neither the arts nor industry. He accepts homage made through them and commands their use: their purpose is to raise souls to heaven and preserve the life of the body here below.

After the Flood, the race of Cham the accursed opened again the paths for civilization; but it is to the children of Shem, to the Chaldeans, to which the glory of the first progress in the highest of natural sciences belongs, which is astronomy.

The first masterpieces of art will be inspired by God Himself, when after having given Moses the detailed plan of the Ark of the Covenant, the tabernacle and everything he had to render, He filled the craftsmen Beseleel and Ooliab with His Spirit so that they were able to imagine all kinds of works of gold, silver, brass, marble, precious stones and wood. (Exodus 31:1-5)

Everything that mythology relates about Opreus and Amphion, everything that history tells of Tyrtaeus is surpassed by David, when by the chords of his harp he calms the evil spirit which agitated Saul and appeases the furies of this unfortunate prince. We have noted the development of music in divine worship through the singing of psalms accompanied by the most varied and harmonious of instruments.

Finally all the arts unite under the hand of Solomon to make the temple of God the wonder of the universe.

Moreover, if history demonstrates that the progress of the arts and industry is mainly due to the religious spirit, it also attests that wherever religion disappears, civilization declines and disappears. Where have the splendours of the Orient been since the hand of Mohammed rested on those opulent lands? Commerce languishes there along with industry; the fine arts are as bad as the cultivation of the soil; death has replaced life.

In the West, first the Reformation, then the Revolution overthrew the most notable monuments of genius in the arts: the temples and the palaces, the altars and the thrones. Browse our museums; you will find lined up there as if in a vast necropolis, the masterpieces of painting and sculpture that have been snatched from the furious hands of Protestant or Revolutionary vandalism; but there they no longer shine with the brilliance they once received from the very buildings for which they were intended by the artist to occupy.

Today, as in the time before the Flood, there are giant peoples whom the vulgar take for the personification of power and glory: "These are the mighty men of old, men of renown", - *'isti sunt potentes a saeculo, viri famosi'.* (Gen. 6:4) These giants now are heretical peoples, schismatic or indifferent in matters of religion, and the simple ones cry out: "Look! Impiety and irreligion bring good fortune!"

"Break through the wall,"- *'Fode parietem'*, (Ezekiel 8:8) said the prophet. And we pierced the wall, and behind these appearances of grandeur and prosperity, what did we see? Within these nations so proud of their civilization all things appeared to our eyes: first of all, bankruptcy and pauperism, so much then for material happiness. Next, divorce: there goes the happiness of the family. At last, suicide: so much for personal happiness.

Such is the 'civilizing progress' promised by the people reformed by Luther, Calvin, Henry VIII, and the people revolutionized in the name of 'the immortal principles and the conquests of 1789'.

The Just One

Plato, so to speak, engraved a portrait of a just man, and he discloses features which makes one believe that he had knowledge of the Holy Books. But, surprising as it is, the justice of Plato remains below the justice of Solomon. Open the book of Wisdom: it is the portrait of Jesus Christ; and such is the precision that one would say it was a painting made after the fact.

In the time of Plato as in the time of Solomon, in the time of Jesus Christ as in the time of Pius IX, the ungodly are the same. Then, as today, they said: "For our time is as the passing of a shadow, and there is no going back of our end: for it is fast sealed, and no man returneth. Come therefore, and let us enjoy the good things that are present, and let us speedily use the creatures as in youth. Let us crown ourselves with roses, before they be withered: let no meadow escape our riot. Let none of us go without his part in luxury: let us everywhere leave tokens of joy: for this is our portion, and this our lot. Let us oppress the poor just man, and not spare the widow, nor honour the ancient grey hairs of the aged. But let our strength be the law of justice." (Wisdom 2:5-11)

"Let us therefore lie in wait for the just, because he is not for our turn, and he is contrary to our doings, and upbraideth us with transgressions of the law, and divulgeth against us the sins of our way of life. He boasteth that he hath the knowledge of God, and calleth himself the son of God." (Wisdom 2:12-13)

By this double trait you recognized Jesus Christ Who never ceases to repeat that His doctrine is not His, but that of His Father, that is to say, that of God: "As the Father hath taught me, these things I speak," (John 8:28). "I speak that which I have seen with my Father," (John 8:38). "I and the Father are one ... Do you say of him whom the Father hath sanctified and sent into the world: Thou blasphemest, because I said, I am the Son of God? If I do not the works of my Father, believe me not. But if I do, though you will not believe me, believe the works: that you may know and believe that the Father is in me, and I in the Father." (John 10: 30, 36-38)

Finally when He is in effect circumvented by His enemies, He is summoned by the high priest to declare if He is the Christ, the Son of God. He replies: "I am," - *'Ego sum,'* (Mark 14:62).

There he is, this righteous man, announced by Solomon, whom the impious will pursue because He had called Himself the Son of God.

But these traits do not just apply to Jesus. Those whom Jesus Himself calls His brothers and to whom He has entrusted His doctrine, these also claim to possess the doctrine of God. It has been given to them to become by grace and adoption what Jesus is by nature, it has been given to them to become the sons of God; "Behold what manner of charity the Father hath bestowed upon us, that we should be called, and should be the sons of God. Therefore the world knoweth not us, because it knew not him," - *'ut filii Dei nominemur et simus'* (1 John 3:1) So the ungodly united against them and circumvented them with a fury reminiscent of the rage of the enemies of Jesus.

One would almost say that the author of the Book of Wisdom attended the assemblies of the Jews in the time of Jesus Christ, also the impiety clubs of the 19th century, and that he stenographed all their speeches: such is the fidelity with which he reproduces their most salient features. Look: this is what those impious say of the Just One, (Wisdom 2:14-20):

"He is grievous unto us, even to behold: for his life is not like other men's, and his ways are very different. We are esteemed by him as triflers, and he abstaineth from our ways as from filthiness, and he preferreth the latter end of the just, and glorieth that he hath God for his father. Let us see then if his words be true, and let us prove what shall happen to him, and we shall know what his end shall be. For if he be the true son of God, he will defend him, and will deliver him from the hands of his enemies. Let us examine him by outrages and tortures, that we may know his meekness and try his patience. Let us condemn him to a most shameful death."

I repeat, could we not say that Solomon must have heard the Jews as they passed in front of the cross, this instrument of shame and torment, while they insulted the ignominies and sufferings of Jesus, saying; "If thou be the Son of God, come down from the cross ... He trusted in God; let him now deliver him if he will have him; for he said: I am the Son of God,"? (Matt. 27:40,43)

Today impiety uses absolutely the same language, and wherever it finds itself powerful enough, impiety treats the Church, the priest, the Pope and the just, in a word, as Caiaphas and the Synagogue treated the Just One *par excellence* - the Son of God. "May God deliver them all now," all the voices say again, "for they say: I am the priest of Jesus Christ, I am the Vicar of Jesus Christ, I am the Church of Jesus Christ; and Jesus Christ is the Son of God, Jesus Christ is God, Jesus Christ is the King!"

God did not deliver Jesus from the cross where the Jews had nailed him; but He delivered Him from the tomb where they believed they had sealed Him up forever.

All you modern Caiaphases, Herods and Pilates: you await for a victorious outcome of your plots, of your contempt and of your abandonment with regards to Jesus crucified in the person of His Vicar whom you have figuratively nailed to the cross by your laws passed against the freedom of his action,[56] and whom you believe confined forever in the tomb of the

---

56   Again, a reference to Bl. Pius IX, the 'prisoner of the Vatican'.

Vatican: "Let us prove what shall happen to him, and we shall know what his end shall be." (Wisdom 2:17) History, however, has told you, and you know how things ended for Jesus and for those who were subjected by you and your like to interrogations of reproach and torment. Just a little while longer, and you will know it again.

<u>Emmanuel</u>

Let us return to our examination of the Scriptures. The infernal power is growing on earth, and the people of God are getting weaker day by day. Out of twelve tribes, ten separated from the tribe of Judah and the royal family of David that is destined to give the world the Messiah and Saviour. Taken into captivity by Shalmanazar, they disappeared forever. Only Judah and Benjamin remain. A little while longer, and these two tribes may also disappear in their turn within the vast empire of Babel. This is a bad time to sing the glories of the coming Saviour, the Son of Judah, the Son of David. Never, in human terms, was the advent of this Universal King more impossible, and therefore more improbable. However, it is at this very time that Isaiah, opening the series of the great prophets in the Old Testament, begins to celebrate the coming of the Offspring of Jesse, His life, His battles, His triumphs, His reign, and this in a tone of assurance and with a precision in details which would make the sacred writer be taken for a historian

of Jesus Christ and of His Church rather than for a prophet.

The book of Isaiah should be quoted in full, but we will limit ourselves to a few features. Let us go back to the time of the prophet. All nations, except one, worship false gods. The people who alone recognize the true God will be absorbed into the bosom of a pagan empire, and it is then that with a boldness which must have seemed like pure madness, Isaiah announces the elevation of the only true God and the complete ruin of idolatry: "And the loftiness of men shall be bowed down, and the haughtiness of men shall be humbled, and the Lord alone shall be exalted in that day," - *'Et elevabitur Dominus solus in die illa; et idola penitus conterentur'* (2:17-18) This day, it is true, has not yet shone in all its splendour; but nevertheless it rises, and it grows from hour to hour. Idolatry, which in the time of Isaiah, constituted the religion of civilized peoples, recedes more and more into the darkness of barbarism, and the prodigious efforts of impiety only serve to enhance the sole sovereign Lord of the earth and the heavens.

Moreover, the prophet had announced something even more surprising and more incredible. "Behold" he cries, "a virgin shall conceive, and bear a son, and his name shall be called Emmanuel." - *'Ecce Virgo concipiet et pariet filium, et vocabitur nomen ejus Emmanuel'.* (7:14) Could we not say that it was as if Isaiah was present during the exchange between the Archangel Gabriel and the Virgin Mary, when we see that in the same terms the heavenly envoy announces to the daughter of David that she will conceive and conceive a son Who will be named Jesus and Who will be called the Son of the Most High?

This is because for Isaiah the future is already present. "For a child _is_ born unto us," he cries again; "and a son is given to us, and the government is upon his shoulder: and his name shall be called, Wonderful, Counsellor, God the Mighty, the Father of the world to come, the Prince of Peace. His empire shall be multiplied an there shall be no end of peace." (9:6-7) On the day when she celebrates the birth of the little Child of Bethlehem, the Church is pleased to repeat these words of the angels which find such manifest fulfilment in this Prince of peace Who came to give it to all men of good will: "Glory to God in the highest; and on earth peace to men of good will," - '_pax hominibus bonae voluntatis_' . (Luke 2:14)

The little Child will grow up. Isaiah sees a rod, that is, a sceptre springing from out of the root of Jesse.   From the mouth of this new Lord springs a word which, like a rod, strikes the earth, and from His lips escapes a breath, which exterminates the impious: "And there shall come forth a rod out of the root of Jesse, and a flower shall rise up out of his root ... He shall strike the earth with the rod of his mouth, and with the breath of his lips he shall slay the wicked. (11: 1-4). Jesus, in fact, without any other sceptre than His word and by the breath of His lips alone, overthrew pagan impiety. It will be the same with the impious of contemporary times.

It is true that the Word of this Conqueror must be supported by works which will be both gifts and miracles. "_God himself will come and will save you,_" says the prophet, "then shall the eyes" of the blind be opened, and the ears of the deaf shall be unstopped. Then shall the lame man leap as a hart, and the tongue of the dumb shall be free." (35: 4-6)

The Prophet Isaiah

One day, John the Baptist will send his disciples to ask Jesus if He is the Messiah: "Are you the one who is to come, or whether we should wait for another?" For all answer Jesus, in the presence of these messengers, healed a multitude of cripples, and He said: "Report to John what you have seen and heard: the lepers are healed, the deaf hear, the dead are raised, the poor are evangelized." (Matt. 11:4-5) It seems that Jesus is quoting the prophet: but, to fulfil that prophecy, *one had to be God.*[57]

The current times are bad you say! It is true. However, no more so than the time when the Messiah appeared. At last He came, this Son of David Whose coming seemed impossible. He was born, this little Child, and for nineteen centuries He has not stopped growing. There will therefore also come that day when the Lord alone will rule and dominate, when the new idols that modern industry and power offer to the civilized people of the present century will be reduced to dust: "The Lord alone shall be exalted in that day. And idols shall be utterly destroyed." - *'Et elevabitur*

---

57   John the Baptist knew the Messiah was already among them, "but there hath stood one in the midst of you, whom you know not ... the latchet of whose shoe I am not worthy to loose," (John 1:26-27), and he knew that Jesus was the Messiah, for he saw the Holy Spirit descend upon Him and reveal that He was God's beloved Son. "And I saw, and I gave testimony, that this is the Son of God." (John 1:34) It would seem St. John sent his disciples on this 'quest' to ask a question he already knew the answer to so that they would come to the realization Jesus was indeed the Messiah. The answer was for them, not for him! Of course, Jesus saw what St. John did, and, 'played along' so to speak, giving them the reply that the prophecies of Isaiah were being fulfilled before their very eyes by Him, and, if they had eyes to see, it would take God Himself to fulfil these prophecies as Fr de Boylesve points out, "For God Himself will come to save you." (Isaiah.35:4)

Dominus solus in die illa; and idola penitus conterentur.' (Isaiah 2-17-18)

<u>The Revolution and the Church</u>

And you, deceitful and mocking men who with a sneering smile on your lips and with rage in your hearts, "ye scornful men" - *'viri illusores'*, (Isaiah 28:14) who believe you dominate the people of God, the Church of His Christ: "who rule over my people that is in Jerusalem," - *'qui dominate super populum meum who is in Jerusalem'*; (Isaiah 28:14) you have said according to Isaiah: "We have made an alliance with death, we have made a covenant with hell,"- *'percussimus doedu cum morte et cum inferno fecimus pactum'*. (28:15) Nothing could be more true; you have made an alliance with the Revolution, and you have declared yourself the defenders of its principles and its ideas; and then you cried out: "When the overflowing scourge shall pass through, it shall not come upon us: for we have placed our hope in lies, and by falsehood we are protected. "- *'Flagellum inundans, cum transierit, non veniet super nos: quia posimus mendacium spem nostram, et mendacio protecti sumus.'* (Isaiah 28:15) – For now what you say is true. Yes, you lied to both the Church and the Revolution because you promised your assistance to both, hoping that when the scourge of the Revolution overwhelmed all shores it would respect you as its most faithful servants and pass over you. But the hope that rests on lies is itself a deception. You believe you have made an alliance of security with the Revolution. Wrong. The

Revolution does not see you as its allies, it only sees slaves. So you may rest assured: the Revolution will not kill you. You serve her too well. *But* when you have served her, or rather, when she has used you to the point of wearing you out and you are of no further use, then ... . No, even then she will not strike; you are not worth it. The dagger, the bullet, the scaffold would be too great an honour for you. She will abandon you. You will go and die somewhere, despised ... . No, not even that; you will simply be forgotten. Remember the Henry IVs and the Frederick IIs of Germany, the Henry VIIIs, the Elizabeths and the Cromwells of England, and others. You have unleashed the tiger; and so the tiger will have a tiger's gratitude for you. (Written and printed in 1861.)

Listen, however, to the history of this new people of God, of this Jerusalem, of this Church that you pretended enslave. "Behold," said the Lord, "Behold I will lay a stone in the foundations of Sion," (28:16) This stone is Jesus Christ: '*petra autem erat Christus*' (1 Corinthians 10:4). This stone is a tried and tested stone - '*lapidem probatum*', (Isaiah 28:16). Jesus was put to the test of poverty, of contradiction, of pain, of reproach, of the whip, of thorns, of nails, of the cross. Nothing could shake Him, and until His last breath He called Himself the King, He called Himself the Son of God. And so He is. This stone is the cornerstone: '*angularem*', (Isaiah 28:16) placed at an angle; it is the key to the vault, and it joins the two parts of the building, the Old and the New Testaments, that is, the synagogue and the Church: "Who hath made both one," - '*faciens utraque unum*'. (Ephesians 2:14) This stone is the foundation of the foundation itself: "founded in the foundation" - '*in fundamento fundamentum*'. (Isaiah 28:16) Observe how Christ truly is the foundation in the foundation. Another stone rests on Jesus, that is, on His Word, a rock that He Himself placed and on which He built His Church: "Thou art Peter; and upon this rock I will build My church," - *'Tu es Petrus, et super hanc petram aedificabo Ecclesiam meam'*, (16:18).

These tall and proud men, who gave themselves the mission of building societies and constitutions, rejected this Stone, the only One that has truly proven Itself, the only One that, even now, has held against the pride of despots and against the storm of revolutions. The rejected has has become nothing less than the head of the corner: "The stone which the builders rejected; the same is become the head of the corner,"- *"Lapidem quem reprobaverunt aedificantes, his factus est in caput anguli.'* (Psalm 117:22)

Jesus appears, and He applies to Himself what the prophets said about this astonishing stone. (Matt 21:42 and Luke 20:17): then He adds a warning, which was prophetic then, and has proved true today: "Whosoever shall fall upon that stone, shall be bruised: and upon whomsoever it shall fall, it will grind him to powder." (Matt. 21:44 and Luke 20:18)

Then, we have before us the one whom Jesus chose to take His place in this world, and for this He named him Peter. Here we have Peter addressing the great Council of the Jews, confirming this stone: "Be it known to you all, and to all the people of Israel, that by the name of our Lord Jesus Christ of Nazareth, whom you crucified, whom God hath raised from the dead, even by him this man standeth here before you whole. This is the stone which was rejected by you the builders, which is become the head of the corner." (Acts 4:10-11). This stone that you rejected from the building has become the key to the vault. Ah! How formidable is this stone! Why has Israel suffered a double death: a religious death and a national death? "Why so" - '*Quare*?' Asks St. Paul. – "For they stumbled at the stumbling-stone", (Romans 9:32). It is because they struck against the stumbling stone, that is, the stone of scandal. '*Offenderunt in lapidem offensionis*'. (Romans 9:32) "As it is written: Behold I lay in Sion a stumbling-stone and a rock of scandal," (Romans 9:33) Isaiah had announced it: "He shall be a sanctification to you. But for a stone of stumbling, and for a rock of offence to the two houses of Israel, for a snare and a ruin to the inhabitants of Jerusalem," (8:14). And what was this scandal? What was this offence? The Jews wanted a conquering Messiah in the manner of the Alexanders or the Caesars; but Jesus, Who is more than Solomon, is also more than Alexander and Caesar. He does not want just bodies, He wants souls. The Jews did not understand, and for them Jesus was a scandal: "But we preach Christ crucified, unto the Jews indeed a stumbling-block," - '*Judaeis quidem scandalum*'. (1 Cor. 1:23) The wise and the powerful understand no better than the Jews did of the wisdom and power of this Wise and Powerful One Who presents Himself to rule without any sword other than the His Word. This Word according to St. Paul is a mystery to them: "Behold I lay in Sion a stumbling-stone and a rock of scandal; and whosoever believeth in him shall not be confounded." - '*Et omnis qui credit in eum non confundetur*'. (Romans 9:33). "Behold, I lay in Sion a chief corner stone, elect, precious. And he that shall believe in him, shall not be confounded. Honour then to you who believe." - '*vobis autem honor credentibus*'. (1 Peter 2:6-8). "But for those who do not

The Cornerstone

believe," continues the Prince of the Apostles, summarizing what David, Isaiah, Jesus Christ, St. Paul and what he himself have already said about this Mystical Stone, "the stone which the builders rejected, the same is made the head of the corner: And a stone of stumbling, and a rock of scandal, to them who stumble at the word, neither do believe, whereunto also they are set." (1 Peter 2:7-8)

A warning to the wise, to the philosophers, to the learned: every doctrine, every science, every word opposed to the Word, that is, opposed to the Stone on which the Church rests is necessarily false and vain — *it will perish.* What we have left to us regarding reason and natural enlightenment can only lead us to wisdom and virtue on the condition that we rise to faith in Jesus Christ, outside of Whom there is no longer any salvation, including for our intellect. "Neither is there salvation in any other. For there is no other name under heaven given to men, whereby we must be saved," - *'Non est in alio aliquo salus'*. (Acts 4:12)

A warning to princes and legislators: every State, every Constitution, every law that does not rest on Jesus Christ, on His Word, on His Church — it will perish. For apart from Jesus Christ, there is no salvation: "Neither is there salvation in any other" - *'Non est in alio aliquo salus'*. And indeed, since the time of Jesus Christ, what is history but one vast picture of the fall and ruin of all those who have stumbled against the stone? Outside and apart from the Church, that is to say, outside the stone on which Jesus Christ built His Church, what do you see? A stormy sea, for the Revolution continues. Two powers are vying for the rule of empire and will continue to do so until the final hour of the ages sounds: on one side there is Lucifer or the Revolution; on the other side, Jesus Christ or the Church.

O you who made a pact with the dead, hoping that death would respect you and pass you by, your pact will be erased in your blood: "And your league with death shall be abolished," - *'Et delebitur pactum vestrum cum morte.'* (Isaiah 28:18)

You have made a treaty with hell. "We have entered into a league with death, and we have made a covenant with hell." (Isaiah 28:15) Insane! Might as well build on a volcano.   Nothing that rests on crime will stand: "Your covenant with hell shall not stand, when the overflowing scourge shall pass, you shall be trodden down by it," - *'et pactum vestrum cum inferno non stabit. Flagellum inundans, cum transierit, eritis ei in conculcationem.'* (28:18)   The scourge of the Revolution, which overflows and passes by, will carry you away with it, you first of all and only you who have declared yourself the servant of the Revolution, and, the propagator of what you so foolishly call its ideas. What foolishness! The flood, after overthrowing you, will tumble you into the mire.

<u>The Saviour</u>

"The voice of one crying in the desert: Prepare ye the way of the Lord, make straight in the wilderness the paths of our God. Every valley shall be exalted, and every mountain and hill shall be made low, and the crooked shall become straight, and the rough ways plain. And the glory of the Lord shall be revealed, and

The Voice in the Desert

all flesh together shall see, that the mouth of the Lord hath spoken." (Isaiah 40: 2-5)

The mountains and the hills, that is, the haughty heights and the grandeurs of the social world were lowered at the word of Jesus; the valleys, symbolic of the basest conditions, were raised by faith and charity. The twisted paths of fraud and lies have been straightened by Christian candour. The detours and rough ways characteristic of pagan politics are only found among men or nations who have lost their Catholic senses. Serpentine finesse only gets what it deserves: universal contempt. The road to virtue once offered so many rough edges along its path so to speak, that, outside of the people of God, there were barely a few men of honour and probity to be found. However, since the arrival of Jesus Christ: the justice of an Aristides, the continence of a Scipio, the fidelity of a Regulus, the devotion of a Codrus, the poverty of a Cincinnatus, the disinterestedness of a Fabricius, are common things among the Christian peoples. Pagan antiquity cites only one martyr for the truth, Socrates, while the martyrs of the Christian faith must be counted in the millions.

Is this surprising? The prophet continues: "Here is your God:" - '*Ecce Deus vester*'; - "Behold the Lord God shall come with strength, and his arm shall rule: Behold his reward is with him and his work is before him." (40:9-10). His work: it is the Church; the reward is heaven, or rather it is He Himself. He gives Himself to those who line up under His banner.

"Fear not ... behold all that fight against thee shall be confounded and ashamed, they shall be as nothing, and the men shall perish that strive against thee." (Isaiah 41: 10-11, and following.) Where are the persecuting Caesars? Where are the contradictory sophists! Where are they? "Thou shalt seek them, and shalt not find the men that resist thee ," - '*Quaeres eos et non invenies,*" (41:12) All that has been done, all that has been said for the Church, subsists and remains. Everything that was said, everything that was done against the Church fades and disappears. "Fear not, thou worm of Jacob, ... I have made thee as a new thrashing wain, with teeth like a saw: thou shall thrash the mountains, and break them in pieces: and shalt make the hills as chaff. Thou shalt fan them, and the wind shall carry them away, and the whirlwind shall scatter them." (41:14-16) It is still the history of those mountains of power or of sophist-geniuses who meet up on the path of the Church and who seek for a way to block its path.

"Behold my servant," notice it is God Who speaks here, "I will uphold him: my elect, my soul delighteth in him: I have given my spirit upon him, he shall bring forth judgement to the Gentiles." (Isaiah 42:1)

Now open the New Testament: Jesus is baptised and a Voice is heard from Heaven: "This is my beloved Son, in whom I am well pleased." (Matt. 3:17) At that very moment the Holy Spirit descended upon Him in the form of a dove, He rested on Jesus, and Jesus immediately began to preach justice.

"He shall not cry out", the prophet continues - '*Non clamabit*', (Isaiah 42:2) Clamouring is a trait of helplessness or weakness. Jesus speaks with the calmness and power of a soul that possesses itself and that dominates: "For he was teaching them as one having power," - '*tanquam potestatem habens*.' (Matt.7:29) So no one can inspire fear in Him; "He shall not ... have respect to person," - *'neque accipiet personam.'* (Isaiah 42:2) While terrible to the great, to the Pharisees, to the scribes whose pride He despises, He is tender and good to sinners; and as little as their good will remains, He receives them, He raises them up. "The bruised reed he shall not break, and smoking flax he shall not quench." (Isaiah 42:3) To the furies of the enemy He opposes with a calm and serene front. Nothing can bring Him down, nothing can disturb Him: "He shall not be sad, nor troublesome," - *'non erit tristis neque turbulentus.'* (Isaiah 42:4) Without turning away from the obstacles, He will continue His work until "He set judgement in the earth," - *'donec ponat in terra judicium,'* (42: 2-4).

"I the Lord have called thee in justice," says the Lord addressing the Messiah, "And I have given thee for a covenant of the people, for a light of the Gentiles: That thou mightest open the eyes of the blind, and bring forth the prisoner out of prison, and them that sit in darkness ... ." (Isaiah 42:6-7)

Indeed, where is light, where is true freedom? What blindness in those nations and in individuals who do not believe in Jesus Christ! What enslavement among peoples and individuals who do not recognize Jesus Christ as their first King!

"Have not I the Lord, and there is no God else besides me? A just God and a saviour, there is none besides me." - *'Deus justus et salvans non est praeter me.'* (Isaiah 45: 21) "Be converted to me, and you shall be saved, all ye ends of the earth: for I am God, and there is no other. I have sworn by myself, the word of justice shall go out of my mouth, and shall not return, For every knee shall be bowed to me, and every tongue shall swear. " (45:22-24) Woe to those who resist him! They will be brought to confusion: "And all that resist him shall be confounded." - *'Et confundentur omnes qui repugnant ei.'* (45:25)

Now, speaking to Sion, "Lift up thy eyes round about, and see all these are gathered together, they are come to thee, ... for thy deserts, and thy desolate places, and the land of thy destruction shall now be too narrow by reason of the inhabitants, ... the children of thy barrenness shall still say in thy ears: The place is too strait for me, make me room to dwell in. And thou shalt say in thy heart: Who hath begotten these? I was barren and brought not forth, led away, and captive: and who hath brought up these? I was destitute and alone: and these, where were they?" (Douay-Rheims, Isaiah 49: 18-21)

(Fr. Marin de Boylesve's text as translated from the French has the following: "Lift up your eyes, O Sion, and look around you. See all these peoples gathered around your ramparts; your deserts now will be too narrow to hold the number of your children; and the sons you begot, when you thought yourself barren, will make these complaints ring in your ears: We lack space; give us, O mother, give us space. Then you will say in your heart; Who gave me these children? Me, struck by sterility, driven from my own home and captive for so long. And these, who fed them? I was abandoned, I was alone, and where were these?")

How can we not recognize in this language the new people of God, the new Sion, the Church of Jesus Christ? But do you want an explanation for this astonishing and sudden fertility? Listen to the prophet: "Thus saith the Lord God: Behold I will lift up my hand to the Gentiles ..." Then look at Calvary: from the top of His cross Jesus extended His hands to all nations. The prophet continues: "... I and will set up my standard to the people." History attests that there is not a known people to whom the apostles and missionaries have not presented the cross. (Isaiah 49:22)

"And kings shall be thy nursing fathers, and queens thy nurses: they shall worship thee with their face toward the earth, and they shall lick up the dust of thy feet. And thou shalt know that I am the Lord, " (Is. 49:23)

Open your history books: since the time of Constantine, there was not a great king nor a great queen who has not made it a duty to support the Church and defend it.   But those foolish politicians, those impertinent lawyers who dare to judge the Church, God will judge them: "But I will judge those that have judged thee, and thy children I will save," - *'Eos vero qui judicaverunt te, ego judicabo'*. (Is. 49: 25)

Let us forget them - how I desire it! - the Balthasars and the Antiochuses, the pagan Caesars, the Senate and the people of Rome, the Henry IVs and the Fredericks of Germany, the Henry VIIIs and the Elizabeth Is of England, the Philip the Fairs of France. They judged the Church, and God judged them. Only yesterday the ministers of the Church appeared at the tribunal of the Revolution.   We know what the judgement was.   But soon the judge-executioners began to devour each other in the Reign of Terror; we saw them staggering, drunk with blood; this blood was no longer that of the priests, it was theirs.   Isaiah predicted it: "And I will feed thy enemies with their own flesh: and they shall be made drunk with their

own blood, as with new wine: and all flesh shall know, that I am the Lord that save thee, and thy Redeemer the Mighty One of Jacob." (49:26)

The Patient One

But the combat must come before the triumph. "I have given my body to the strikers, and my cheeks to them that plucked them: I have not turned away my face from them that rebuked me, and spit upon me. " (Isaiah 50:6)   Is this Isaiah speaking, or the Evangelist? Let us listen to St. Matthew: "Then they spat in his face and beat him, and they smote him, saying Prophesy, Christ, and say who smote you." (Matt. 26:67-68)

"There is no beauty in him, nor comeliness. And we have seen him, and there was no sightliness, that we should be desirous of him." (Isaiah 53: 2)

There He is: "despised, and the most abject of men, a man of sorrows, and acquainted with infirmity: and his look was as it were hidden and despised, whereupon we esteemed him not. Surely he hath borne our infirmities and carried our sorrows: and we have thought him as it were a leper, and as one struck by God and afflicted. But he was wounded for our iniquities, he was bruised for our sins ... by his bruises we are healed. All we like sheep have gone astray ... and the Lord hath laid on him the iniquity of us all. He was offered because it was his own will." (53:2-7)

Everything is in accordance with this. Jesus declares that he is the Good Shepherd Who will lay down His life for His sheep, and will give it freely: "I lay down my life, that I may take it again.   No man taketh it away from me: but I lay it down of myself, and I have power to lay it down: and I have power to take it up again." (John 10: 17-18)

And above all, He offered Himself because He *wanted* to. He did not allow Himself be caught, for with a word He overthrew the soldiers who had come to arrest Him. Then, when delivered to torments that should have caused His death twenty times over, He does not die: this is because no created power can take His life: "No man taketh it away from me," - *'Nemo tolli eam a me'*. (John 10:18)

When He does die in the end, it while uttering a loud cry that any other dying person experiencing such a loss of blood and with that amount of suffering would naturally have been incapable of doing. Therefore, when He dies, it is because He wants to: "I lay it down of myself," - *'Sed ego pono eam a meipso.'* (John 10:18) Thus is verified the prophecy of Isaiah (53:7): "He was offered because it was his own will,"- *'Oblatus est quia ipse voluit'*.

"And he shall not open his mouth," to complain. (Is. 53:7)   Slandered, outraged, jeered at, beaten, scourged, crowned with thorns, nailed to the cross, Jesus does not let out a complaint, not a word, not a sigh. Isaiah predicted: "he shall be led as a sheep to the slaughter, and shall be dumb as a lamb before his shearer, and he shall not open his mouth", - *'et non aperiet os suum'*. Is this not Jesus before the judges and under the hand of His executioners? "But Jesus held his peace,"- *'Jesus autem tacebat'*. (Matt 26:65)

"And the Lord was pleased to bruise him in infirmity: if he shall lay down his life for sin, he shall see a long-lived seed ... because he hath delivered his soul unto death, and was reputed with the wicked. " (Is. 53: 10-12)   See Jesus crucified between two thieves, after having been compared with an assassin, to Barabbas, who was then preferred over Him: "And was reputed with the wicked," - *'et cum sceleratis reputatus est.'*

"He hath borne the sins of many, and hath prayed for the transgressors." (Ibid.) We know that the first words of Jesus on the cross were a prayer. These words of Jesus on the cross were a prayer for his executioners. "Father, forgive them, for they know not what they do."

At last, enough with suffering, enough with shame. The heroism of this dedicated sacrifice calls for the glory of triumph. "Behold I have given him for a witness to the people, for a leader and a master to the Gentiles." (Isaiah 55:4) "Arise, be enlightened, O Jerusalem: for thy light is come, and the glory of the Lord is risen upon thee. For behold darkness shall cover the earth, and a mist the people: but the Lord shall arise upon thee, and his glory shall be seen upon thee. And the Gentiles shall walk in thy light, and kings in the brightness of thy rising." (Is. 60:1 etc.)

What a night, what a darkness indeed, what ignorance hovers over those peoples and individuals who stand outside the influence of the Church of Jesus Christ! On the contrary, what splendour, what glory surrounds the nations and kings that the Church illuminates with its rays!

To Serve or Perish

But now the prophet takes a more proud and bolder tone. "Thy gates," he says, addressing Jerusalem, "shall be open continually: they shall not be shut day nor night, that the strength of the Gentiles may be brought to thee, and their kings may be brought." (Is. 60:11) "For every nation, every kingdom that will not serve you, will perish," -'*Gens enim et regnum quod non servierit tibi, peribit.*' (60:12)

If we look back at the time when Isaiah appeared, we cannot be surprised enough by the audacity of such language. This prophecy was made shortly before the dispersion of the Jewish people in the provinces of the empire of Nebuchadnezzar. Once again, the timing was ill chosen to declare that every nation, every kingdom that did not serve Jerusalem would perish. However, this seemingly rash statement has become a *fait accompli.*

Rome refused to serve Jerusalem, and old pagan Rome disappeared with its Caesars, its Senate and its heathen people; while afterwards the new Jerusalem was established in Rome and from there to extend over the world an empire which exceeds all the limits of that of ancient Rome.

The Rome of the East, Constantinople, refused obedience to the leader of new Jerusalem and the new Rome. Thus the reign of the patriarchs and the Caesars, which first became the Lower Empire, ended up disappearing.

Where are these German, English or French dynasties which stood against the Jerusalem of Jesus Christ? "For every nation, every kingdom that will not serve you, will perish,"- *'Gen et renum quos non servierit tibi, peribit.'*

But, it is pointed out that certain powers on earth are still standing, that they even seem to be growing since they refused to serve the living Jesus Christ in the Church. Isaiah already anticipated this objection, and he responded. Be still, be patient: this apparent greatness of theirs is only pride. "It is pride only, sit still." – *'Superbia tantum est, quiesce.'* (30:7) These nations imagine themselves to possess strength because they possess gold and iron. They say they are happy, because they live in luxury and have good food. They forget that a nation is not merely a material or animal assembly, but a meeting of intelligent and free beings.   So already these so-called high and great powers are staggering like drunken men. The Lord mixed in their drink the spirit of sleep, and their eyes are closed. "For the Lord hath mingled for you the spirit of a deep sleep, he will shut up your eyes, ... And the Lord said: Forasmuch as this people draw near me with their mouth, and with their lips glorify me, but their heart is far from me, and they have feared me with the commandment and doctrines of men. ... Woe to you that are deep of heart, to hide your counsel from the Lord: and their works are in the dark, and they say: Who seeth us, and who knoweth us?" (Isaiah 29:10-15) Their policy, their diplomacy, their militia are struck by blindness.   All the wisdom of these clever men consisted in playing one against the another, and the one who knew how to best deceive prevailed for a time; but, the one who prevailed by by dint of lying, he has now been worn out; the mocker is done with him: "For he that did prevail hath failed, the scorner is consumed," - *'Defecit qui praevalebat, consummatus est illusor.'* (Isaiah 29:20) (September 4, 1870!!!)[58]

Rise up, O Sion! "And the children of them that afflict thee, shall come bowing down to thee, and all that slandered thee shall worship the steps of thy feet," (Isaiah 60:14)   The entire chapter should be transcribed here to give an idea of the triumphs promised to Sion, figure of the Church. You ask how the thing will be done; where is this triumph, especially in our times? For example, in 1861, the year when we first wrote these lines, or in 1870, the time when we rewrote them, or finally in 1875, the time when we reprinted them?[59] Where is the man, where is the nation that will avenge the Church for the universal desertion of current governments and peoples, and

---

58   Fr de Boylesve is referring to the establishment of the Third Republic of France on this date and the end of the reign of Louis-Philippe, aka Napoleon III (1808-1873), nephew and heir to Napoleon I. Louis-Philippe had been approached by the French royal family to be regent until the rightful heir to the throne, Henry V, was of age. Instead, with backing from the French Assembly, Louis-Philippe was made a constitutional king. He was the only President (1848–52) of the French Second Republic and, as Napoleon III, the Emperor (1852–70) of the Second French Empire. Thus, he had helped to end the legitimate absolute monarchy in France after its short-lived restoration while also usurping the throne, and, compelled Henry to go into exile. Now, the very powers that he had sold out to in order to gain the throne had turned on him. The Third Republic that was formed after his reign collapsed during the Franco-Prussian war, hence, the reference to 'the scorner is consumed'. Also, see Fr de Boylesve's biography at the beginning of this book.

59   Obviously, this text is the third reprint: Fr de Boylesve is asking where is the promised triumph during all these years of revolutionary and anti-clerical political upheaval in Catholic France?

who will restore its influence and its empire over nations and over kings? God will find him. A man of little or no means is enough for His purpose; but above all He delights to take up an abandoned man, unrecognised, forgotten in the desert, a David also forgotten in the fields where he feeds the flock, then hunted like a wild beast by a jealous king. Such a man is chosen; he is a Mattathias, a hundred-year-old old man; he is a Constantine exposed to a thousand pitfalls, a Theodosius withdrawn far from the court; he is a Pelagius entrenched in the mountain; he can also be a Charlemagne already seated on a throne. But whoever God takes by the hand, as long as he lets himself be led and obeys, listening to those secret voices that speak to him and that he alone hears just like St. Joan of Arc did - against him all the perfidies of politics are in vain, and the dagger is as powerless as the cannon blast. The chosen man at the right hand of the Lord is small, always small in some way, but he is worth a thousand. He is alone, alone like Moses before Pharaoh and Israel, alone like Leo the Great before Attila and Genseric, alone like Gregory VII before the German Caesar, alone like Pius IX before the Revolution; but he is stronger than the multitude and the strongest nation; "The least shall become a thousand, and a little one a most strong nation:" -'*Minimus erit in mille et parvulus in gentem fortissimam.*' (Isaiah 60:22).

When will this man appear? When will this salutary turnaround take place? When? At the marked time: '*in tempore ejus*.' How? Suddenly: '*Subito*' - "I the Lord will suddenly do this thing in its time," – '*Ego Dominus, in tempore ejus subito faciam istud*.' (60:22)[60]

---

60   Once more, we cannot help but observe a pointed reference to the hope that God will raise up a new deliverer – aka, the exiled Great Catholic Monarch of prophecy.   One might even dare say this was a hidden note of encouragement not only to the Catholics of the time, but even perhaps to Henry V himself to not lose hope considering Fr de Boylesve has just compared the end of Louis-Philippe's reign with the wicked ones of Isaiah's prophecy, i.e. the scorner that prevailed for a time, but was eventually consumed.

In 1873 to the astonishment and bewilderment of many, including Pius IX, Henry made a bold stand with his Declaration of the White Flag upholding the absolute Catholic Monarchy of France; he refused to make the least compromise with the Revolution by rejecting the offer dangled before him by the National Assembly in that he would regain his throne by accepting the Tricolour and a constitutional monarchy. Henry preferred to stay in exile rather than accept the throne under the conditions of the Revolution. He refused to sell out like Louis-Philippe had done. This was an act of 'insanity', even Bl, Pius IX couldn't understand Henry taking such a stand over a white 'napkin' and losing the throne in the process, but, we may dare venture a guess that Fr de Boylesve was one of Henry's supporters and one of the very few who understood why Henry made such a bold and insane declaration at the time, insane to the eyes of the eyes of the world that is.   Notice that Fr de Boylesve had already demonstrated earlier that when defending the Church and God's royal right of kingship, it is a fight for the truly zealous. Just like Moses, one must not make the least compromise and sell out, no matter how small or insignificant the compromise may seem, not one iota, *not 'one hoof' should be left behind for the Pharaohs of the day, or a flag for that matter!* See

He is Alone

"The sword of the Lord is filled with blood, it is made thick with the blood of lambs and buck goats, with the blood of rams full of marrow: for there is a victim of the Lord in Bosra and a great slaughter in the land of Edom ." (Isaiah 34:6)

"Who is this that cometh from Edom, with dyed garments from Bosra, this beautiful one in his robe, walking in the greatness of his strength?" (Isaiah 63:1)

"I, that speak justice, and am a defender to save ." (Isaiah 63:1)

"Why then is thy apparel red, and thy garments like theirs that tread in the wine press? (Isaiah 63: 2)"I have trodden the wine press alone ... : I have trampled on them in my indignation, and have trodden them down in my wrath, and (the blood of My enemies) is sprinkled upon my garments, and I have stained all my apparel. ... I looked about, and there was none to help: I sought, and there was none to give aid: and my own arm hath saved for me, and my indignation itself hath helped me. And I have trodden down the people in my wrath, and have made them drunk in my indignation, and have brought down their strength to the earth. ... And he said: 'Surely they are my people, children that will not deny,'" (63.1-8)

---

the section-chapter: 'Moses'.

Jesus found Himself alone on the day of the Passion; He still finds Himself alone in the days of the passion of His Church. During the Passion it was He Who was trodden in the press under the feet of His enemies, and, if His robe was red then, it was red with His own Blood. During the passion of His Church, the blood of its martyrs reflects itself on His robe, which is the Church itself. But the turnaround is terrible. The blood of the righteous falls on the head of him who sheds it. The blood of Abel pursued Cain. The Blood of Jesus fell on the Jewish deicides; let us remember the siege of Jerusalem by Titus afterwards and the eleven hundred thousand Jews who perished there. The blood of the martyrs falls on the Caesars and on the persecuting nations. Remember Rome, indignant with the blood of martyrs then in return drowned in its own shame by the barbarian sword. Remember the last days of the Revolution, drunk on the blood of its victims, then in turn drowning in blood as its own slaughtered each other. "And I have trodden down the people in my wrath, and have made them drunk in my indignation," - *'Et conculcavi populos in furore meo et inebriavi eos in indignatione mea.'* (63:6)

Like the Saviour, and like all those great men who before or after Jesus Christ devoted themselves to saving, you will be alone at first. Like Jesus from the top of His cross, you will look around you and there will be no help; you will search, and no one will come forward to help you. '"I looked about, and there was none to help: I sought, and there was none to give aid." - *'Circumspexi, et non erat auxiliator; quaesivi, et non fuit qui adjuvaret.'* (Isaiah 63:5)

And yet, woe to those who do not dare to declare themselves to be for Jesus and with also for those whom He calls to continue His work! He only recognizes as belonging to His people, to His Church, those who recognize Him and will not deny Him:

"Surely they are my people, children that will not deny: so he became their saviour." - 'Verum tamen *populus meus est, filii non negantes.*' (Isaiah 63:8)

Woe to the people who abandon their God and their Saviour, they themselves will be abandoned. "And the city of the Holy One became deserted; Zion was abandoned, Jerusalem was desolate. The house which we had consecrated and which was our glory and in which our fathers offered you their praises, this temple has fallen prey to the flames, and everything we loved has turned into ruins." (64:10-11) Twice the first people of God brought this punishment upon themselves, and twice the temple was burned: the first one by Nebuchadnezzar, the second by the Romans. The second people of God, the Church of Jesus Christ, is sheltered from this misfortune: it never abandons its God, and its God never abandons it. But it is not so with nations: there is hardly a single one which does not at certain times abandon Jesus Christ and rise up against the Church. But history attests to the terrible misfortunes that befell these ungrateful and indocile nations.

There are people who, like the Jews, absolutely refuse the faith or to give obedience to Jesus Christ living and speaking in the person of His Vicar. Like nations that fall into heresy or schism, God rejects them as He rejected the Jewish people and replaces them with other people. He had predicted it through the mouth of Isaiah: "They have sought me that before asked not for me, they have found me that sought me not. I said: Behold me, behold me, to a nation that did not call upon my name.' (65:1)

The apostate people are not, however, completely abandoned: for there are always a few souls there who, in the midst of general desertion, remain faithful to their God. Thus among the children of Israel Jesus made a choice of disciples and apostles whom He charged with forming a new people for Him. It seems Isaiah heard Him declare His purpose. "I come that I may gather them together with all nations and tongues: and they shall come and shall see my glory. And I will set a sign among them, " - 'et ponam in eis signum'. (66: 18-19) How can we not recognize the sign spoken of, the standard of the cross, that for so long before had been a cursed sign, a sign of slavery and a symbol of death, which has become the sign of freedom, religion and honour, and which for eighteen centuries has dominated the nations?

Isaiah continues (66): "Among those who have received salvation, I will send to the nations beyond the sea, in Africa, in Lydia, in Italy, in Greece, to the distant islands, to those who have not heard of me and who have not seen my glory, and they will declare my glory to the nations, and they will bring all your brothers," that is to say, those who by faith in the Son of Abraham have become your brothers, they will bring "of all nations as a gift to the Lord, to the holy mountain of Jerusalem," Jerusalem being a figure of the Church, which Jesus compares to a city built on a mountain. – Among these new believers, "I will choose priests and Levites;" and "all flesh shall come and worship before my face. They will see the corpses of those who were unfaithful to me. The worm that gnaws them does not die, the fire that devours them does not go out. All flesh will see their ruin and their torment which will never end," - '*Et erunt usque as satietatem visionis omni carni.*'   This terrible announcement closes the book of Isaiah. And now, powerful enemies of Jesus Christ and of the Church, triumph for now, but know this and do not forget: each has his turn.

All is Lost

In the life of the Church, as in the life of each Christian, joys and sadness, hopes and fears follow one another or even combine together.   Likewise, in the history of the ancient people of God, right after the brilliant announcements of Isaiah come the sad lamentations of Jeremiah.   Likewise also, at this moment, we await and hope for a triumphant future the Church and for France its Eldest Daughter, even while the present times are lamentable, so lamentable even, that all hope seems chimerical.

Let us not let ourselves be overcome. Guilty and miserable as it is, the Christian people are less guilty and less defeated than Jerusalem was at the time when Jeremiah wept over its crimes and its misfortunes. However, even then, absorbed as he is by his pain and by the evils of his times, the prophet glimpses a ray of hope in the future. "The days will come," says the Lord, "I will raise up to David a just branch: and a king shall reign, and shall be wise, and shall execute judgement and justice in the earth. In those days Judah will be saved. ... and Israel shall dwell confidently: and this is the name that they shall call him: the Lord our just one." (23: 5-6) This prediction applies first to Jesus Christ, the only offspring of David Who has reigned since the time of Jeremiah, to Jesus Christ, the Sage One and Just One *par excellence*; but it also applies to those extraordinary men whom God raises up, when He pleases, to continue the work of His Son and to save the people who replaced Judah.

In the meantime, that is, at the time these prophecies were made, the ruin of the people of God is complete. The reign of a son of David and Judah seems impossible. And now, to confound human politics, God desires to announce this coming kingdom with new brilliance.

First of all, this new announcement comes from Baruch, Jeremiah's former secretary. Captive himself with his brothers, he predicted the splendour of Jerusalem which in his day was razed to a heap of ruins. "God," he said, "found out all the way of knowledge, and gave it to Jacob his servant, and to Israel his beloved. Afterwards he was seen upon earth, and conversed with men," - '*Post haec in terris visus est, et cum hominibus conversatus est.*' (Baruch 3:38) "Put off, O Jerusalem, the garment of thy mourning, and affliction ... For God will shew his brightness in thee, to every one under heaven." (Baruch 5:1-3) How can we not recognize here Him Who, being the splendour of the glory of the Father (Hebrews 1:3)[61], and at the same time the Son of David, Who made Himself visible on earth and revealed Himself in the middle of Jerusalem by the brilliance of His doctrine, His miracles and His by the superhuman patience?

---

61   "In these days hath spoken to us by his Son, whom he hath appointed heir of all things, by whom also he made the world. Who being the brightness of his glory, and the figure of his substance." (Hebrews 1:2-3)

"Arise, O Jerusalem, and stand on high: and look about towards the east, and behold thy children gathered together from the rising to the setting sun, by the word of the Holy One rejoicing in the remembrance of God." (Baruch 5:5)

Then it is Ezekiel who, from the in the midst of this same period of captivity, also announces the salvation of the flock that was then scattered like dry bones over the entire surface of the immense Babylonian empire. "And I will set up one shepherd over them, and he shall feed them, even my servant David: he shall feed them, and he shall be their shepherd. And I the Lord will be their God: and my servant David the prince in the midst of them: " (34:23-24) "I will take ... the tribes of Israel ... and I will put them together with Judah, ... and I will make them one nation in the land on the mountains of Israel, and one king shall be king over them all: and they shall no more be two nations. ... they shall be my people, and I will be their God. And my servant David shall be king over them, and they shall have one shepherd." (Ezekiel 37: 19, 22, 24) Since Ezekiel, no son of David other than Jesus could call himself the shepherd and prince of Israel; but also Jesus reigns, in fact, through His Vicar over all those children of Israel and Judah, who by becoming Christians, have become one people. Now this unity of the children of Jacob was only the prelude to the much more vast and much more marvellous unity of all nations under the leadership of the one who Jesus Christ established as the universal shepherd of His lambs and sheep.

In the Time of Nebuchadnezzar

Let us return to the midst of the debris of the ancient people of God scattered across the face of the immense empire of Nebuchadnezzar. Babylon stands triumphant and her dominion seems unshakeable like her ramparts. Indeed, look around the world; search for a nation that is capable of troubling the queen of civilization at that time. Only Nineveh could challenge her for power; but practically gave up the sceptre, never to take it again. – Mede has shaken off the yoke; but it fell again under the strong hand of proud Chaldea. – Further out, I see a harsh and poor nation called Persia. It is not from these unknown and unrecognised people that Babylon expects its master.

Who could disturb the repose of the great Nebuchadnezzar? – The West? - The people on that side of the world seem to have lost enlightenment and intelligence as they moved away from the Sennaar plain and from the regions illuminated by the rising sun. Besides, compared to Asia at the time, Europe hardly seems like a province. It is true that at one of its ends, on a land cut up by the waves of the sea, we see a small people in an agitation as it rises, or rather, we see a confused mass of a very small people differing in origin, name, dialect, genius and character. But in the most heroic time of their history, even when united together, these people took ten years to overthrow a city called Troy, which was not equal to one district of Babylon. Since this one great feat, there is only one important thing for the Greeks, and this is most solemn to them – it is their sporting feats and games!

What can Babylon fear from a nation that resembles children and whose ambition is reduced to competing for the prize of running, wrestling, boxing or pucks? – True, not all is games: we find they speak about a certain Lycurgus, founder and legislator of a large town known in the country under the name of Sparta. But from Sparta to Babylon, from a political point of view even more than from a geographical point of view, what a distance between them! They also talk about a philosopher named Solon, who, more fortunate than a certain Draco,[62] managed to have a set of laws accepted by the simple inhabitants of a dozen towns, that finally united into a single city, Athens, which was thanks to Theseus, the only hero this country has ever had seen. But, from the time when Theseus united the twelve towns of Athens to the time of Draco and Solon, six hundred years passed. And so, since the time of Theseus, for six hundred years those people are still expecting just laws. – It is probable that in the court of Nebuchadnezzar, Athens and Sparta are not even known by name; and so it seems that they in Babylon could then ignore Solon, Lycurcus, Theseus, and even the famous Hercules, the hero of fable, without this

---

62   Draco (c. 625-600 BC) was the first recorded legislator of Athens in Ancient Greece. He implemented the 'Draconian constitution' that was to be enforced by a court of law, replacing the system of oral law and blood feuds. His attempts to change the old blood-feud system obviously required a heavy hand, for it is from his name was receive the word 'draconian'. Solon (c. 630-560 BC) was an Athenian statesman, lawyer, political philosopher and poet. Solon's attempts to legislate against the political, economic and moral decline of the times resulted in reforms that overturned most of Draco's laws. He is one the Seven sages of Greece and credited with laying the foundation of Athenian democracy.

ignorance compromising the reputation of the scholars of Chaldea.

It is also permissible for mighty Babylon to ignore that behind the Hellenic peninsula there is another one called Italy, and that, on one point of this peninsula, a refuge has just been opened to thieves by two brothers, one of whom murders the other for a simple joke about the new city.[63] Rome, this is what this cluster of cabins is called, Rome will also embark on its own siege like that of Troy.[64] It will take it ten years to overcome a city that would not be the twentieth part of Babylon. Tell Nebuchadnezzar that one day Rome will surpass in power and grandeur his

---

63   There are several variations on the legends of the founding of Rome by the two brothers Romulus and Remus. Generally, the legends states the brothers fought over the location of the foundation of their new city; Romulus chose the Palatine Hill, while Remus desired the Aventine Hill. In order to settle the matter, they agreed to consult an augury of birds. Each brother prepared a sacred space on their hills and began to watch for birds. Remus claimed to have seen six birds, while Romulus said he saw twelve birds. Romulus asserted that he was the clear winner by six birds, but Remus argued that since he saw his six birds first, he was the winner. They continued to quarrel until Romulus began building walls around his chosen hill: the Palatine Hill. In response to this construction, Remus made continuous fun of the wall and his brother's city, even jumping over the wall as a mocking jest. In response to Remus' mockeries, Romulus killed him. He then built his city, but, Rome's initial population was supplied by fugitives, exiles, runaway slaves, and criminals and other outcasts.

64   The Siege of Veii, (c. 505 – 496 BC). Veii was an early rival of ancient Rome, and the Romans warred for ten years to overcome it. At the time, Rome was still in a very early form of development and its citizen-militia was a far cry from the professionalized legions that the Roman empire would later have.

great, mighty Babylon!   Nebuchadnezzar would respond with an amused smile.

Above and beyond the borders of Italy, mountains rise and forests stretch out, and under their shadows hide a people doomed to eternal darkness. They would at least think so in Babylon, for even the star-diviners of the Chaldea have not yet glimpsed in the heavens the destiny of those far off nations which will one day be France, Spain, England, and Germany.

Let us not even try to cross the ocean. In the age of Nebuchadnezzar, Babylon had nothing to fear from either of the Americas, whose existence it probably did not even suspect.

Let us return to Asia. Babylon can still extend its conquests there. Apart from the Mede, who is no longer a cause for concern, and Persia who is not a concern either, there remain the Scythian, the Indian, Arabian and the Chinese peoples.

The nomadic Scythian can escape the yoke of another ruler, he can, like the torrent in the day of a great flood, cover for a moment the banks of the Tigris and the Euphrates; but an overflow of a population is not an empire. – India and Arabia are in the service of Babylon, while China is still waiting for its Confucius. Moreover, separated from the rest of Asia by deserts and almost impassable mountains, China of that time can no more dispute the rule of empire with Babylon than receive it itself.

Therefore, on the evening when Nebuchadnezzar was lying on his bed and pondering about about what would happen here below after his reign, he could not even suspect that Babylon would ever lose the sceptre of the civilized world. Also, who in July 1870 would have dared to tell Paris that it could falter?[65] Therefore, much more foolish would the one appear to be who would announce to Nebuchadnezzar that the power of Babylon could have an end. The proud monarch therefore dreamed, and he only dreamed of ever-increasing the glory for his great Babylon.

But on that evening, God made him see something else.

The Four Metals

Nebuchadnezzar therefore thought about the future. Suddenly he sees a gigantic statue standing in front of him. The head of the colossus was of gold, the chest and arms of silver, the belly and thighs of bronze, the legs of iron, and the feet part of iron and part of clay. Nebuchadnezzar looked on. And now, without the help of any hand, a stone comes loose from the side of a mountain which, rolling, hits the feet of the statue. Immediately the colossus collapsed; the clay, iron, bronze, silver and gold, reduced to powder, were carried away by the wind, and there was no trace left. But the stone that had toppled the image became a mountain and covered the whole earth.

---

65   France was the predominant power in Europe, until the Franco-Prussian war, which broke out that month and year, and would eventually bring about the unification of Germany and make it the predominant power, much to Fr de Boylesve's dismay. See his biography in "About the Author".

Daniel Shown the Meaning of Nebuchadnezzar's Dream

Such was the dream of Nebuchadnezzar, and here is the explanation of the prophet Daniel. The gold represented the empire of Nebuchadnezzar; the silver, that of the Persians. The bronze, that of the Greeks; the iron, that of the Romans.

Gold, the most precious of the metals, is the instrument of magnificence. Greatness was the hallmark of the Assyrian genius.

Silver is the instrument of corruption and enslavement *par excellence*, because "all things obey money," - *'pecuniae obediunt omnia'*. (Ecclesiastes 10:19) In the struggle of the Persians against the Greeks, money played the main role.

The sonorous tone of brass recalls this noisy people of the Greeks whose oratorical and poetic language still catches our ear.

Iron, terrible as it is useful, represents the people who worked the land and were soldiers, a nation as adept at wielding hoes as well as their swords, and that skill made this people king.

But in the end, the clay, which is the mud of corruption, mixed with the Roman iron.

Then, without any help from the hand of man, a stone was detached from Mount Sion. This "rock was Christ": - *'petra autem erat Christus'*, (1 Corinthians 10:4), this stone was the one on which Jesus Christ built His Church: "That thou art Peter; and upon this rock I will build my church,". *'tu es Petrus et super hanc petram aedificabo Ecclesiam meam.'* (Matt. 16:18) Struck by this stone, the Roman colossus collapsed, only the memory remains.

Four empires successively dominated everything civilized in the world, but there will be no other universal monarchy than that of Jesus Christ. When these kingdoms have had their day, Daniel said, "The God of heaven will set up a kingdom that shall never be destroyed, and His kingdom shall not be delivered up to another people, and it shall break in pieces, and shall consume all these kingdoms, and itself shall stand for ever." - *'et ipsum stabit in aeternum.'* (Daniel 2:44) By this feature you recognized the One Whose eternal Kingship the angel will announce. "Behold," says St. Gabriel to the Virgin, "thou shalt bring forth a son ... the Lord God shall give unto him the throne of David his father; and he shall reign in the house of Jacob for ever. And of his kingdom there shall be no end." - *'et regni ejus non erit finis'.* (Luke 1:31-33)

The Four Animals

Daniel in turn receives a vision (Daniel, Chapter 7). The world appears to him in the form of an immense sea, agitated by the four winds of the heavens. From the bosom of the waves emerge four gigantic animals, one right after the other.

The first looked like a lioness, but it had the wings of an eagle. The lion and the eagle hold the pride of place among the animals: the first, the lion holds pride of place on the earth, while the second, the eagle, holds the air. This exalted rank is as gold is among all the metals. This is still representative of the pride of the Assyrian empire; it is also a sign of voluptuous softness: because the animal seen by Daniel is not a lion, it is a lioness.

The second giant animal looks like a bear. Its mouth is armed with a triple row of teeth. This beast is told: "Arise, devour much flesh." We recognize here

the Persians, rough and austere like the country from which they come. "Devour much flesh" - Persia is to conquer the empire of Babylon. The triple row of teeth represents the triple nations that makes up the army of Cyrus: the Persians, the Medes and the Armenians.

The third animal rushes forward, similar to a leopard, but armed with wings like a bird. Is this not Alexander rushing with the Greeks, supple, varied, and sober, but terrible and as quick as the leopard? Would not one say that they had wings, so rapid was their flight? - The beast had four heads. The Empire of Alexander will divide into four monarchies: Thrace, Macedonia, Syria and Egypt.

However, the night is getting darker. The fourth beast appears, terrible, astonishing, excessively strong: - '*Ecce bestia quarta terribilis atque mirabilis, et fortis nimis.*' Its mouth is armed with iron teeth. This beast eats and crushes, trampling underfoot what its leaves - '*comedens atque comminuens, et reliqua pedibus conculcans.*' It does not look anything like the previous ones.

Rome, in fact, does not resemble Greece, nor Persia, nor Assyria. Remember, its people are iron: "iron teeth"- '*dentes ferreos*'; terrible, astonishing, robust. Nebuchadnezzar, Cyrus, Alexander are content to subjugate people and impose governors and tribes on them. Rome does more: it assimilates and incorporates the people it conquers and transforms them into Romans. So she devours and crushes them, or else she annihilates them under her feet, as she did with Carthage. Her empire surpasses all previous ones: "The fourth beast shall be the fourth kingdom upon earth, which shall be greater than all the kingdoms, and shall devour the whole earth." - '*Bestia quarta regnum quarium erit in terra, quod majus erit omnibus regnis, et devorabit universam terram .*'

The animals of Daniel's dream are in accordance with the metals of Nebuchadnezzar's dream.

The prophet continues: "I beheld till thrones were placed, and the Ancient of Days sat: his garment was white as snow, and the hair of his head like clean wool: his throne like flames of fire: the wheels of it like a burning fire. A swift stream of fire issued forth from before him."

What is this throne of the Ancient of Days, if not the subtle, brilliant and rapid element which, under the name of light and fire, is like the first agent which God uses to impart movement to matter?   And what are these wheels? Are they not the solar systems that turn in the heavens like the wheels of the chariot of the Eternal?

Daniel continues: a thousand thousand angels served Him, and ten thousand times a hundred thousand assisted Him.   The Judge sat down, and books were opened. Power was taken away from these formidable beasts, the face of human empires.   And behold, carried on the clouds, the Son of Man came and ascended to the Ancient of Days. And He was offered in His presence; and the Ancient of Days gave Him power, honour and royalty; all people, all tribes, all languages will serve Him; His power is an eternal power which will never be taken away from Him; and His kingdom will never perish.

Yet the prophet sees a horn rising up against the Saints, and prevailing over them for a time. - Do not be frightened when a horn, at first small (Piedmont, Prussia), grows and stands up insolently; that it speaks against the Most High, that it imagines that it can change times and laws (7:25). Its time is marked: it in turn will be crushed and it will perish, so as not to appear again.   It is the story of Antiochus, the impudent, the deceitful, the foolish.   So when in the West, as formerly in the East, iniquities have grown, '*cum creverint iniquitates,*' (8:23) there will arise a king whose impassive face will know no shame: "There shall arise a king of a shameless face, - '*consurgt rex impudens facie*;' a king intelligent in the art "understanding dark sentences," that is, of deception:

'intelligens propositiones' (8:23). "His power will be strengthened, but it will not rest on his own force." (8:23) The power of the Antiochus of the West will rest on the forces of the Revolution. It will devastate everything beyond belief. Indeed, it took the spectacle of the universal demoralization of recent times to understand to what extent a man with an impudent face can corrupt everything that his influence touches. Thanks to this corruption, he will succeed, and he will do whatever he wants against the people of the Saints : deceit will be his weapon, "craft shall be successful in his hand," - *'dirigetur dolus in manu ejus'*, (it is always Daniel who speaks, 8:25), and at the same time in the end he will rise against the Prince of princes. But God is waiting for him there. At the moment when, by a perfidious abandonment, he handed over the sovereign Pontiff, he himself fell, crushed without firing a shot: *'et sine manu contereretur'*. (Daniel 8:23-25) History speaks like prophecy: and the history of the Antiochus of yesterday only guarantees us of the fate of the Antiochus of today.[66]

---

66   Again, it seems that Fr de Boylesve may have seen a parallel between Daniel's biblical prophecy foretelling the rise of the Antichrist, and the reign of the usurper Napoleon III who took the French throne from the true king, Henry V and ended the absolute Catholic Monarchy, thus heralding the separation between Church and state. However, Napoleon III was not completely unsympathetic towards the Holy Father as he did send French troops to support the Papal forces threatened by Garibaldi and his fighters. Nevertheless, he withdrew the troops when the Franco-Prussian war broke out in 1870 as those forces were needed, which allowed Rome to be overtaken, thus he may have been seen as 'abandoning the Pope' according to Fr de Boylesve's pointed comment. And, he got what he deserved according to him as we saw in an earlier note: Napoleon III lost the Battle of Sedan, and the Revolution he compromised with 'abandoned' him too in the

The Messiah

Daniel never ceased to beg the Lord to bring an end to the captivity of his people. The Archangel Gabriel is sent to him and he announces both the restoration of Judah and that of the entire human race. Let us listen to him:

"The seventy weeks of years have been shortened for the sake of your people and the holy city, so that transgression may end, that sin may be put to an end, iniquity may be blotted out and replaced with everlasting righteousness, that the visions and prophecies be fulfilled, and that the Holy of holies receive the anointing. Know therefore and observe carefully. From the decree which will be made for the restoration of Jerusalem until the coming of Christ, the Prince, there will be seven weeks and sixty-two weeks (of years). After sixty-two weeks, Christ will be put to death. The people who have denied Him will not be His. Another people will come under the leadership of a leader, and he will destroy the city and the sanctuary. The war will end in terrible devastation, and afterward will come the predicted desolation (by Moses, Isaiah and the other prophets)." (Daniel 9:24-26)

- (The Christ) will confirm his covenant with many in one week (of years), and in the middle of the week the host and the sacrifice will cease. The abomination of the desolation will last until the consummation and until the end. (Daniel 9:27)

---

end with the establishment of the Third Republic, ending his constitutional monarchy.

In a few words, so many details! The coming of Christ, His work, His death and the time of His death: "And after sixty-two weeks Christ shall be slain," - *'Et post hebdomades sexaginta duas occidetur Christus;'* (v. 26). The destruction of His people who will deny Him: "And the people that shall deny him shall not be his." (v.26, etc.) - *'Et non erit ejus populus qui eum negaturus est'.* The ruin of Jerusalem and the temple, "And a people with their leader that shall come, shall destroy the city and the sanctuary: and the end thereof shall be waste," - *'Et civitatem et sanctuarium dissipabit populus cum duce venturo'.* The devastation and desolation already predicted by Moses, Isaiah, Jeremiah, Ezekiel: "And after the end of the war the appointed desolation." - *'Et finites ejus vastitas, et post finem belli statuta desolatio'.* The confirmation of the Divine alliance with men, the cessation of the sacrifice of the old law in the middle of a 'week' of years, which places the immolation of the Saviour after the first three years of His preaching: "and in the half of the week the victim and the sacrifice shall fail," - *'Et in dimidio hebdomadis deficiet hostia et sacrificium'.* Then, the abomination of the desolation in the temple: "There shall be in the temple the abomination of desolation," - *'Et erit in templo abominatio desolationis'.* Finally, the desolation of the deicide people until the end of the world: "And the desolation shall continue even to the consummation, and to the end," - *'Et usque ad consumptionem et finem perseverabit desolatio'.*

The scriptural commentators have noted that all these facts were accomplished in the order that the angel had marked.

The Agreement between the Prophets

The four great prophets agree on the battles, the triumphs and the Reign of the Saviour promised and expected since the beginning of time. Those we designate under the name of 'minor' prophets' are no less formal.

Osee (Hosea) predicted the conversion of foreign nations to the one that God will be pleased to call His people: "I will say to the people who were not mine: 'You are my people,' and these people will say: "Thou art my God", (Osee 2:24)   St. Paul and St. Peter demonstrate the fulfilment of this prophecy in the vocation of the Gentiles to the faith of the true God. (Romans 9:25, 1 Peter 2:10)[67]

Joel (2:28) announces the outpouring of the Holy Spirit on all flesh. On the day of Pentecost this marvel begins to come true. St. Peter points out this fact at the same time as he himself fulfils the prophet's prediction (Acts 2:16 etc.).

Jonah is thrown into the sea to calm the storm; he remains three days and three nights in the belly of

---

67   "Even us, whom also he hath called, nor only of the Jews, but also of the Gentiles. As in Osee he saith: I will call that which was not my people, my people; and her that was not beloved, beloved; and her that had not obtained mercy, one that hath obtained mercy." (Romans 9:25) – "But you are a chosen generation, a kingly priesthood, a holy nation, a purchased people: that you may declare his virtues, who hath called you out of darkness into his marvellous light: Who in time past were not a people: but are now the people of God. Who had not obtained mercy; but now have obtained mercy." (1 Peter 2:10)

an enormous whale. Deposited on the shore, he will preach penance in Nineveh, capital of the largest pagan empire of that time. Thus, Jesus is sacrificed to appease Divine Justice; after three days and three nights spent in the bosom of the earth, He resurrected, and He sent His apostles to preach penance to the pagan world. Therefore, when He was summoned by the Jews to give a sign of His divine mission, He declared that they would have no other sign than that of the prophet Jonah. This symbolism of the resurrection was so well understood that, after the death of Jesus, His enemies declared to Pilate: "This seducer said while he was alive: I will rise again three days after my death." - We know the success of their preventative manoeuvres around the tomb of their Victim. It will be the same in all times. Let us remember Pius VII in Savona.[68] What a lesson for those now around Pius IX in the Vatican!

Micheas (Micah) describes the future dominion of the God of Jacob: "In the last day the house of the Lord will rise like a mountain on the top of the mountains and all peoples will flock to it. And the nations will hasten, saying; Come, let us go up to the mountain of the Lord, to the season of the God of Jacob; and he will teach us his ways, and we will walk in his paths: for the law will go out of Sion, and the word of the Lord out of Jerusalem." (4:1-2) – The Church indeed dominates everything that is highest in this world. For eighteen centuries, nations have continued to flock there. The word of Jesus Christ and his law came out of Jerusalem from where the apostles departed.

This prophet saw the place where the Messiah was to be born: "And you, Bethlehem, are small among

---

68   See footnote 15.

the cities of Judah; it is from you (however) that He who will rule in Israel will come; (but) his origin goes back to the beginning, to the days of eternity." (5:2)

Such was the clarity of this prediction that on the arrival of the Three Magi Herod consulted the doctors to know where the Messiah was to be born, and they answered without hesitation: "In Bethlehem," immediately confirming their answer by the text of Micheas. (Matt. 2:5 -etc.)

"A little while longer," says the Lord, by the voice of Aggeus (Haggai) (2:7), "I will shake heaven and earth, and the sea and the barren land; I will shake all the people, and then the Desired of the nations will come," - *'Et veniet Desideratus cunctis gentibus.'* At the time preceding the birth of Jesus Christ, all nations were shaken by the 'shock' of Pompey, Caesar, Brutus, Antony and Octavian, who on land and sea, competed for the empire. The victory of Octavian, who became Augustus, restored calm and Jesus came into the world.

The new temple, erected by the Jews on their return from captivity, did not equal the magnificence of the old one. "Who is left among you, that saw this house in its first glory? How do you see it now? In your eyes, is it not nothing in comparison?" (Aggeus 2:4) Nevertheless, Aggeus announced that the glory of this new house will erase that of the first: "Great shall be the glory of this last house more than of the first, saith the Lord of hosts," - *'Magna erit gloria domus istius novissimae plus quam primae,* dicit Dominus exercituum'. (2:10) "There," says the Lord of hosts, I will give peace." - *'Et in loco isto dabo pacem, dicit Dominus exercituum.'* - The new temple, in fact, will receive within its walls the true Solomon, the Prince of peace, Jesus Christ the Saviour of the world.

Zechariah summarizes the most brilliant prophetic depictions of Isaiah. He sees the fall of the empires of the world, the glory and the expansion of Jerusalem. It is then that at last the Saviour rises: "For behold I will bring my servant the Orient," - *'Ecce enim ego adducam servum meum Orientem'* (3:8) His name is, 'the man who rises': "Behold a man, the orient is his name: and under him shall he spring up, and shall build a temple to the Lord." (6:12) What is this temple, if not the one of which St. Paul often speaks and of which we are the living stones, the Church of which Jesus Christ is the Head?

"Rejoice greatly, O daughter of Sion, shout for joy, O daughter of Jerusalem: behold thy king will come to thee, the just and saviour: he is poor, and riding upon an ass, and upon a colt the foal of an ass. " (9:9) You can recognize the triumphal entry of Jesus into Jerusalem. It was then that he spoke kindly to some Gentiles, as Zechariah had spoken: "He shall speak peace to the Gentiles," - *'Et loquetur pacem gentibus.'* - (9:10). Then also Jesus predicted at the same time the fall of the world and His own triumph; "At this hour the prince of the world will be cast out; and I, when I am lifted up from the earth, will draw all things to Myself." (John 12:32) This is what Zechariah saw: "His power will extend from sea to sea, and from the river to the ends of the earth." (9:10).

Jesus Christ attributes this power to the sacrifice of the cross: "When I am lifted up from the earth, I will draw all to Myself." Zechariah had announced that through the Blood of His testament He would deliver the captives from the pit where there is no water: "Thou also by the blood of thy testament hast sent forth thy prisoners out of the pit, wherein is no water."

- *'Tu quoque in sanguine testmenti tui emisisti vinctos de lacu in quo non est aqua.'* (9:11) Is not this

the Blood of Christ, the Blood of the New Testament, shed for men and for the remission of sins? (Matt. 26:28) "For what is the marvel of his goodness, except the wheat of the elect and the wine that makes virgins?" - *'Quid enim bonum ejus erit, et quid pulchrum ejus nisi frumentum electorum et vinum germinans virgines'*? (9:17) And this wheat of the elect, this wine so pure? What else is this if it is not the Bread changed into the Body of Jesus, and the wine changed into His most Adorable Blood?

Jesus, however, will be sold at a low, mean price. Thirty denarii, that is His value in the eyes of the traitor and the buyers: "And they weighed for my wages thirty pieces of silver." - *'Et appenderunt mercedem meam triginta argenteos'.* (Zacharias 11:12) Could we not say that the prophet was present at the infamous deal made by Judas? "What will you give me," he said to the chief priests, "and I will deliver him to you. And they agreed on thirty denarii," - *'at illi constituteunt ei triginta argenteos.'* (Matt. 26:15) Zechariah even saw the use that would be made of these thirty denarii. "And the Lord said to me: Cast it to the potter ... that I was prized at by them. And I took the thirty pieces of silver, and I cast them into the house of the Lord to the potter." (11:13) See Judas bringing back the thirty pence, throwing them into the house of the Lord. What will they do with it? They held a council, and they decided that with this money they would buy a potter's field for the burial of foreigners. (Matt. 27:3, 5- 6). Thus the thirty denarii, the price of treason, will go into the hands of the potter. This is what the prophet announced.

Now, go on to Calvary. See the crowd around the cross. As one they contemplate the One they have pierced and crucified. St. John sees this: "And again another scripture saith: They shall look on him whom they pierced." (19:37) It was Zecharias who predicted it: "And they shall look upon me, whom they have pierced," - *'Et aspicient ad me quem confixerunt.'* (12:10) Others weep. St. Luke tells of this: "And all the multitude of them that were come together to that

Judas Returns the Money

sight, and saw the things that were done, returned striking their breasts."(23:48)   Zecharias had announced this as well: "And they will mourn for him as one mourns for an only son; they will grieve as one grieves over the death of a firstborn," (12:10).

"And they shall say to him: What are these wounds in the midst of thy hands? And he shall say: With these I was wounded in the house of them that loved me." (Zecharias 13:6) Was not Jesus nailed to the cross by those who should have been His most zealous defenders?

"Strike the shepherd," the prophets continues, "and the sheep shall be scattered." (13:7)   Jesus Christ applies to Himself and to His apostles this prediction of which at the same time He in turn announces the next fulfilment: "All you shall be scandalized in Me this night. For it is written: I will strike the shepherd, and the sheep of the flock shall be dispersed." (Matt. 26:31)   This double prophecy happened only too soon. Barely is Jesus in the hands of His enemies when His flock abandons Him and flees: "Then the disciples all leaving him, fled," -'*Tunc discipuli omnes, relicto eo, fugerunt.*' (Matt. 26:56)

Finally the universal reign of Jesus Christ is formally announced by Zechariah as by the other prophets: "And the Lord, he says, will be King over the earth: in that day there will be only one master." (14:9) This has not yet been seen to its complete fulfilment, but, will be seen when the ruin or conversion of all the people who fought against the new Jerusalem takes place. This solemn prediction closes the book of Zechariah's prophecies.

The last prophets of the old law will not be any less formal. Through Malachias' mouth, God complains of the contempt shown to Him by the children of Israel in the choice of victims they offer in sacrifice. "Who is there among you, that will shut the doors, and will kindle the fire on my altar gratis? I have no pleasure in you, saith the Lord of hosts: and I will not receive a gift of your hand. For from the rising of the sun even to the going down, my name is great among the Gentiles, and in every place there is sacrifice, and there is offered to my name a clean oblation: for my name is great among the Gentiles, saith the Lord of hosts." (Malachias 1:10-11)

Take a look around the globe. Every day, at every hour of the day, from dawn to sunset, as the sun rises, a pure Victim is offered to the true God. Because the Church of Jesus Christ sends its priests everywhere, and everywhere the Eucharistic Sacrifice is offered.

The correspondence between Malachais' prophetic announcement and the celebration of the Eucharistic Sacrifice alone would be sufficient to demonstrate at the same time both the inspiration of the prophet and the Divine institution of the holy Mass.

Malachias is the last of the prophets of the ancient law; he foresees the first of the prophets of the new law, the one of whom Jesus will say that he is more than a prophet. Also Malachias calls him 'the angel' - "Behold, says the Lord, I will send my angel, and he will prepare the way before you." (3:1) We recognize the one whose voice Isaiah heard crying in the desert: "Prepare the way for the Lord: make his paths straight."

Let us conclude here with Malachias: "I am the Lord and I do not change," - *'Ego Dominus et non mutar.'* (3:6) Compare with Numbers (23:19) "God is not a man, that he should lie, nor as the son of man, that he should be changed.[**] Hath he said then, and will he not do? hath he spoken, and will he not fulfil?" Immediately after the Fall of man, He promised a Saviour. Since then, He has repeated His promise a hundred times over. It was therefore necessary that the Saviour came at the time, and in the manner of the times and circumstances foretold: "I am the Lord," -*'Ego Dominus;'* and God does not change: *'Et non mutar'*. – And, the marked time of the prophecies meets precisely at the time when Jesus Christ appeared on earth. Jesus Christ, moreover, brings together in His person and in His works all the features indicated by the prophets: through Him and in Him alone is the entire Old Testament verified. – Jesus Christ is therefore the Saviour promised and awaited since the fall of Adam.   Meanwhile, however, a great scandal shakes faith and shatters hope. Look around you. Happiness and power on this earth are the prerogative of those nations and individuals who are distinguished by their indifference or even by their very hatred towards Jesus Christ and of His Church. Then, on the contrary, misfortune and weakness become the privilege of the most faithful servants of Him Whom the prophets present to us as the King of peoples and of kings.

Don't speak so! But, this has been predicted as well. Yes, it was predicted what I have just said. Listen

____

[**]   That is, He is not like us, corrupted mankind born in sin – men sin, lie, cheat, and go back on their promises. God is incorruptible, cannot lie, and is faithful to His word and promises.

again to Malachi: "You said: 'He laboureth in vain that serveth God, and what profit is it that we have kept his ordinances, and that we have walked sorrowful before the Lord of hosts? Wherefore now we call the proud people happy, for they that work wickedness are built up, and they have tempted God and are preserved.' " (3:14-15)

But it is also foretold by Malachias that we will see how the righteous and the ungodly differ from each other, between the one who serves God and the one who does not serve Him. "And you shall return, and shall see the difference between the just and the wicked: and between him that serveth God, and him that serveth him not: (3:18) -- "Then they that feared the Lord spoke every one with his neighbour: and the Lord gave ear, and heard it: and a book of remembrance was written before him for them that fear the Lord, and think on his name. And they shall be my special possession, saith the Lord of hosts, in the day that I do judgement: and I will spare them, as a man spareth his son that serveth him." (3:16-17) -- "For behold the day shall come kindled as a furnace: and all the proud, and all that do wickedly shall be stubble: and the day that cometh shall set them on fire, saith the Lord of hosts, it shall not leave them root, nor branch." (4:1) "But unto you that fear my name ... you shall go forth, and you shall tread down the wicked when they shall be ashes under the sole of your feet in the day that I do this, saith the Lord of hosts." (4:2-3)

Over the past century, we have seen the fulfilment of this prophecy ten times: how many earthly powers have been swept away like ashes for refusing to serve God and His cause!

Prophets remain silent when true philosophers are about to speak. God wants mankind to prove and test itself, and, by His power and mankind's powerlessness at the same time, He wants to demonstrate both the gratuitousness and the necessity of divine revelation.

Gratuitousness of divine revelation: the pagan philosophers Socrates, Plato, Aristotle have shown by their lessons that, even after the Fall, man still has enough reason left to him to recognize the existence of God and the moral law: God was therefore not obliged to grant mankind the revelation of these truths. It was given to mankind freely.

The necessity of divine revelation: now notice that these men, so powerful for their genius, mingled their most beautiful insights with strange errors: therefore, divine revelation was morally necessary for the fallen human race in order to put it back on the road to true wisdom and perfect happiness.

This is the twofold lesson that emerges from philosophy when left to its own devices: a mixture of wisdom and folly, which has always been and which is everywhere on display.

Come then, O Jesus; come, sole Saviour of intelligence and hearts; come, hasten, triumph, advance and reign: "Set out, proceed prosperously, and reign. " *intende, prospere procede, et regna.'* (Psalm 44:5)

<u>He Must Reign</u>

"He *must* reign," (1 Cor. 15:25) such is the cry in which all the great words and all the great deeds which preceded the coming of Jesus are summed up. The voices of centuries to follow will never stop saying the same thing. It will be nineteen centuries since hell and the world have worn themselves out in vain efforts to contradict these three words of the great St. Paul. The most formidable empires have collapsed, the most famous systems have vanished, the most skilfully concerted utopias and constitutions have been swept away by the eagles like cobwebs. How many men, today's giants, are nothing but mere pygmies when compared with the giants of old! What a number of men that have been acclaimed kings of the world and of human thought by the universal suffrage of the masses! After a great clamour of arms or words, they have disappeared, and their memory is scarcely remembered today: "The swords of the enemy have failed unto the end: and their cities thou hast destroyed. Their memory hath perished with a noise," - *'Periit memoria eorum cum sonitu'*. (Psalm 9:7) All those who had the naivety to believe in them were dissipated and destroyed: "And all that believed ... were scattered, and brought to nothing," - *'Et omnes qui credebant ei, dissipati, sunt et redacti ad nihilum,'* (Acts 5:36).

Men of these times, only born yesterday in comparison, why this obstinacy in honouring us with your insults and your attacks? If our mysteries and our faith are dreams, if our miracles are fables, if our

Church is only a human work, and the craziest and weakest work that ever was at that, then leave it alone, this 'old' Church, which is so worn out and decrepit according to you. Yes, it is old, very old, much older than you, although perhaps less worn out than you have said and less so than you would wish; but finally since it is so old and so 'worn out', let alone so it may die a death that cannot take long: "Let them alone; for if this council or this work be of men, it will come to nought," - *'Sinite illos, quoniam si est ex hominibus consilium hoc, aut opus, dissolvetur'*. (Acts 5:38)

But, O men of these times, if our divinely revealed mysteries were so many truths, superior it is true but in no way contrary to the weak reason of man; and if there are miracles which demonstrate the divine revelation of these mysteries and thereby prove their truth, if these miracles were recorded facts and truly superior to the forces of created nature and to the conceptions of human genius and possibly even angelic genius, and therefore only possible to the omnipotence of God and attested by history with as much certainty as the historical exploits of an Alexander or a Caesar — if, to sum it up in a word, that Jesus Christ is God, and if consequently His Church is the work of a God — *then take care.* "If it be of God, you cannot overthrow it, lest perhaps you be found even to fight against God." (Acts 5:39)   The thunder of your bronze and the lightning of your genius may well be powerless to dissolve us: "You cannot overthrow it." Take care; *perhaps it is to God Himself that your blows are addressed.* Be careful, your rages could well, like so many others before you, only confirm the predictions of a prophet whose foresight has not yet been caught in error. If Jesus Christ is God, I repeat, His Church is Divine; and like your predecessors, the Caiaphases and the Neros of yesteryear, you will pass, you and your memory along with the noise of your threats and your thunderbolts: "Their memory hath perished with a noise ... but the Lord remaineth forever"- *'Periit memoria eorum cum sonitu ... Dominus in aeternum permanet.'* (Psalm 9: 7, 8)

It has been well over two thousand years since Isaiah announced the fall of every nation and every power that would not make it a duty and an honour to serve the Church of Jesus Christ: "For the nation and the kingdom that will not serve thee, shall perish," - *'Gens et regnum quod non servierit tibi peribit'.* (60:12) It has been nearly a couple thousand centuries since the Apostle, supporting the prophet, repeated in his turn, and even more clearly: "Jesus Christ, yesterday, and today; and the same for ever," and it is He who will reign in the centuries to come: - *'Jesus Christus heri et hodie; ipse et in saecula'.* (Hebrews 13:8) So it needs be He must reign, He must reign even before the victory is complete, He must reign even at the height of the battle, He must reign as long as He has enemies who resist Him, He must reign until at last He reduces them all to His footstool: "For he must reign, until he hath put all his enemies under his feet,"- *'Oportet autem illum regnare donec ponat omnes inimicos sun pedibus ejus.'* 1 Cor. 15:25) We remember this is what David had announced: "The Lord said to my Lord: Sit thou at my right hand: Until I make thy enemies thy footstool." (Psalm 109) St. Paul and David, the Apostle and the Prophet agree in this; the New Testament confirms the Old, and as the centuries unfold, display the fulfilment of both, converting the prophecies of the reign of Jesus Christ into history through the Catholic Church.

APPENDIX

A Prayer to Christ the King

O Christ Jesus, I acknowledge Thee to be the King of the universe: all that has been made is created for Thee. Exercise over me all Thy sovereign rights.

I hereby renew the promises of my Baptism, renouncing Satan and all his works and pomps, and I engage myself to lead henceforth a truly Christian life. And in an especial manner do I undertake to bring about the triumph of the rights of God and Thy Church, so far as in me lies.

Divine Heart of Jesus, I offer Thee my poor actions to obtain the acknowledgement by every heart of Thy sacred Kingly power. In such wise may the kingdom of Thy peace be firmly established throughout all the earth. Amen.

A Short Prayer to Jesus Christ the King

Almighty and everlasting God, Who in Thy Beloved Son, King of the whole world, hast willed to restore all things anew; grant in Thy mercy that all the families of nations, rent asunder by the wound of sin, may be subjected to His most gentle rule. Who with Thee liveth and reigneth world without end. Amen.

<u>**Prayer for the Conversion of Sinners**</u>
<u>**and the Liberty and Exaltation of the Church**</u>

(From the Leonine Prayers at the End of Low Mass)

O God, our refuge and our strength, look down with mercy upon Thy people who cry to Thee, and through the intercession of the glorious and Immaculate Virgin Mary, Mother of God, of blessed Joseph her spouse, of Thy blessed Apostles Peter and Paul, and of all the saints, mercifully and graciously hear our prayers for the conversion of sinners, and for the freedom and exaltation of holy mother Church. Through the same Christ Our Lord.   Amen

<u>**Consecration of the Human Race**</u>
<u>**to the Sacred Heart by Pope Leo XIII**</u>

Most sweet Jesus, Redeemer of the human race, look down upon us, humbly prostrate before Thine altar.   We are Thine and Thine we wish to be; but to be more surely united with Thee, behold each one of us freely consecrates himself today to Thy Most Sacred Heart.

Many, indeed, have never known Thee; many, too, despising Thy precepts, have rejected Thee. Have mercy on them all, most merciful Jesus, and draw them to Thy Sacred Heart.

Be Thou King, O Lord, not only of the faithful who have never forsaken Thee, but also of the prodigal children who have abandoned Thee, grant that they may quickly return to their Father's house, lest they die of wretchedness and hunger. Be Thou King of those who are deceived by erroneous opinions, or whom discord keeps aloof and call them back to the harbour of truth and unity of faith, so that soon there may be but one flock and one shepherd. Be Thou King of all those who even now sit in the shadow of idolatry or Islam, and refuse not Thou to bring them into the light of Thy kingdom. Look, finally, with eyes of pity upon the children of that race, which was for so long a time Thy chosen people; and let Thy Blood, which was once invoked upon them in vengeance, now descend upon them also in a cleansing flood of redemption and eternal life.

Grant, O Lord, to Thy Church, assurance of freedom and immunity from harm; give peace and order to all nations, and make the earth resound from pole to pole with one cry: Praise to the Divine Heart that wrought our salvation: to it be glory and honour forever.   Amen

Prayers Revealed to Olive Danzé:
Sr. Marie of Christ the King, (1906-1968)

1) Prayer to Merciful Jesus

(On March 3, 1927, Jesus inspired Sr. Marie to write this prayer, saying to her: "Each time this prayer is said, I will attach to it a great blessing and the mark of My Love".)

O Jesus most merciful, through Your Heart pierced by the spear, snatch Your children from the perils of death, slow down the persecutions, unite all Your children, let them all be Your members. Rule over all hearts.

O Universal King, give light to the Leader who represents You. O My Jesus, may your Heart be honoured, known, loved throughout the world!

May the Presence of God be known in the Holy Eucharist!

May all creatures prostrate themselves before Him, the Most High, the Only God!   Amen.

2) Prayer to Christ the King, Prince of Peace, Master of Nations

(Dictated to Sr Marie by Christ Himself)

O Jesus, the only King of the universe,

We prostrate ourselves at Your feet,

To adore You, And to take you for our

King and our Guide.

Yes Lord,
To You all nations are subject,
You alone are the True King,
You alone are true Peace,
You alone are true Light,
We adore You alone.

You are our Only support,
You are our Master,
O Great God of Heaven and Earth.
We believe very firmly that You are really present,
In the Eucharist. You are there, alive, loving.

You want to feed us with the Bread of Life.
Yes, come and feed Your children.

Your gaze is fixed on souls,
You watch over all Nations.
Your Heart is for us a haven of rest,
We therefore consecrate ourselves to Your Heart as
King and Prince.

To You Alone, Lord,
All Glory, Honour, Love, be returned,
Until the consummation

of the centuries and in all Eternity. Amen.

3) A Prayer said by Sr. Marie of the Cross

O Jesus Christ – King, over all nations be also the King of my heart and my soul. O Master of heaven and earth, be master over Your child. O Divine Heart of Jesus, I want to recognize You as my home and delight in Your pleasure. Yes, my Jesus, You are the true God, the only God, Christ-King. O my Jesus, infinitely good for the poor sinners who turn to You, show me Your Heart, open Your Heart to me to hide myself completely so as to see only You alone. O Jesus, I want to love You for those who outrage and despise You in the Holy Eucharist. You are misunderstood, forgotten, well my King, I want to know You and make You known to souls who do not know You. I believe, O my God, that You are truly present in the Holy Host. Amen."

<u>A Prayer for the Triumph of the Catholic Faith</u>

(By Bishop Athanasius Schneider)

Almighty and eternal God, Father, Son, and Holy Spirit, we kneel before Your Majesty, and thank You from the depth of our soul for the inestimable gift of the Catholic Faith, which you have deigned to reveal to us through Jesus Christ, True God and True man. We received this divine light in holy baptism and have promised You to keep this faith inviolate until death.

Increase in us the gift of the Catholic Faith. By Your grace, may it be strengthened and made unshakeable. Daily increase in us the understanding of the beauty and profoundness of the Catholic Faith, that we might live in the deep joy of Your divine truth and be ready to sacrifice all things rather than compromise on or betray this faith. Grant us the grace to be resolved to undergo a thousand deaths for even one article of the Creed.

Graciously receive from us sinners an act of humble reparation for all the sins committed against the Catholic Faith by the laity and clergy, especially by high-ranking clergy who, contrary to the solemn promise they made at their Ordination to be teachers and defenders of the integrity of the Catholic Faith, have become champions of heresy, poisoning the flock entrusted to them and gravely offending the Divine Majesty of Jesus Christ, the Incarnate Truth.

Grant us the grace to see all the events of our life, and the immense trials our Holy Mother Church is now undergoing, in the supernatural light of faith. May we believe that You will cause to arise from today's vast spiritual desert a renewed flourishing of faith that will adorn the garden of the Church with new works of faith and give rise to a new age of faith.

We firmly believe that the Catholic Faith is the one true faith and religion, which you invite every person freely to embrace. Through the intercession of the Blessed Virgin Mary, the destroyer of all heresies, and the great Martyrs and Confessors of the faith, may the Holy, Catholic and Apostolic Faith triumph again in the Church and the world, so that no soul may be lost but rather come to the knowledge of Jesus Christ, the only Saviour of mankind, and through a right faith and righteous life attain eternal beatitude in You, O Most Holy Trinity, Father, Son, and Holy Spirit. To You be given all honour and glory, for ever and ever.

Amen.

FINIS

Illustration Credits

Cover Image. Page 22. *"Christus Consolator"*, by Carl Bloch (1881). Artvee, public domain collection.

Page 31. *"God creates light over the waters."* Wood engraving by Thompson after J. Martin (1789-1854). Wellcome Collection. Public Domain.

Page 32. *"God the Father Creating the World"*, Karl Ferdinand Sohn, (1805–1867). Walters Art Museum – Public Domain listing in collaboration with Wikimedia Commons.

Page 38. *"An Angel Holding a Sword"*, engraving by W. Bromley after P.J. de Loutherbourg, (1793). Wellcome Collection. Public Domain.

Page 41. *"The Archangel Michael"*, Baldassare Franceschini (Italian, 1611-1690). Artvee. Public Domain.

Page 42. *"The Fall of the Rebel Angels"* (1605), Eugenio Cajés (Spanish, 1575-1634). Artvee. Public Domain.

Page 44. *"The Crowned Virgin: A Vision of John"*, etching by Gustave Dore. Wikimedia Commons, Public Domain.

Page 49. *"Satan Exulting over Eve"*, (1795). William Blake (English, 1757-1827). Artvee. Public Domain.

Page 53. *"Cain in the Spell of Satan"*, (1843). Edouard Dujardin (Belgian, 1817-1889) Artvee. Public Domain.

Page 55. *"The Flood, the last of the giants destroyed"*, David Humbert de Superville (Dutch, 1770-1849). Artvee. Public Domain.

Page 59. *"The Tower of Babel"*, (first quarter of the 17th Century) Flemish School. Artvee. Public Domain.

Page 75. *"The Sacrifice of Abraham"*, (ca. 1631 – 1635), Cornelis de Vos (Flemish, 1584 – 1651). Artvee. Public Domain.

Page 77. *"The Crucifixion"*, (1866). Gustave Doré. Wikimedia Commons. Public Domain.

Page 80. *"Religion Enthroned"*, Frederick Stymetz Lamb (American, 1862-1928). Stained glass window Brooklyn Museum, Gift of Irving T. Bush in memory of his father and mother, 29.1082. Creative Commons-BY (Photo: Brooklyn Museum, 29.1082_SL3.jpg).

Page 87. *"Juda"* (shown as the ancestor of the kings and house of David). Etching / engraving. Print maker: Dirck Volckertsz. Coornhert (mentioned on object), after design by: Maarten van Heemskerck (mentioned on object). (1550). Rijksmuseum. Public Domain.

Page 95. *"The Procession in the Streets of Jerusalem"*, (Le cortège dans les rues de Jérusalem), James Tissot. Brooklyn Museum – Wikimedia Commons.

Page 101. *"Moses and Aaron Appear before Pharaoh"*, (1866). Wikimedia Commons. Public Domain.

Page 103. *"The Destruction of Pharaoh's Army"*, (1792). Philippe-Jacques de Loutherbourg (French, 1740 – 1812). Artvee. Public Domain.

Page 110. *"The Egyptians Drown in the Sea"*, (1866). Gustave Doré. Wikimedia Commons. Public Domain.

Page 124. *"The Death of Korah, Dathan, and Abiram."* Gustave Doré – Bible Illustrations. Wikimedia Commons. Public Domain.

Page 129. *"Balaam's prophecy the star of Jacob"*, (Baalam Prophétise Qu'un Astre S'élèvera Du Milieu D'israël) – (1858). Artvee. Public Domain.

Page 132. *"La Transfiguration; La Résurrection du Christ"*, (1874). Camille Félix Bellanger (French, 1853 – 1923). Artvee. Public Domain.

<u>Page 141.</u> *"Christ Mocked"*, Gustave Doré. Illustration from "The Bible panorama, or The Holy Scriptures in picture and story (1891)". Wikimedia Commons. Public Domain.

<u>Page 151.</u> *"Christ the King"*, by Gonzalo Carrasco, (1859-1936). Frick Digital Collections. Public Domain.

<u>Page 160.</u> *"King David"*, (1868). Arnold Böcklin (Swiss, 1827-1901). Artvee. Public Domain.

<u>Page 164.</u> *"The construction of the ark of Noah."* Colour lithograph by L. Gruner after N. Consoni after Raphael, (1483-1520). Wellcome Collection. Public Domain.

<u>Page 172.</u> *"The Annunciation"*, (1890). Carl Bloch (Danish, 1834-1890). Artvee. Public Domain.

<u>Page 175.</u> *"Isaiah"*, (c. 1838). Ernest Meissonier (French, 1815-1891). Artvee. Public Domain.

<u>Page 181.</u> *"The Corner Stone"*, (Le pierre angulaire), by James Tissot. (Created: between 1886 and 1894). Brooklyn Museum Collection - Wikimedia Commons. Public Domain.

<u>Page 184.</u> *"The Voice in the Desert"*, (La voix dans le désert) by James Tissot. (Created: between 1886 and 1894). Brooklyn Museum Collection, listed as public domain courtesy of the Brooklyn Musem.

<u>Page 190.</u> *"Christ with Crown of Thorns"*, (Christus mit der Dornenkrone). Aelbrecht Bouts, (ca 1505). Artvee. Public Domain.

<u>Page 200.</u> *"The agony of Christ in the garden of Gethsemane; an angel descends to strengthen him while cherubs hover with the instruments of the Passion."* Engraving by C. Bouzonnet Stella after J. Stella. Wellcome Collection. Public Domain.

<u>Page 206.</u> *"The Door of the Fold"*. Illustration from "A book of mortals; being a record of the good deeds and good qualities of what humanity is pleased to call the lower animals", (1905). Internet Archive Book Images - Wikimedia Commons. Public Domain.

Page 213. *"Daniel is shown the interpretation of the king's dream",* (1873). Illustration from "The Story of the Bible from Genesis to Revelation", Wikimedia Commons. Public Domain.

Page 216. *"Daniel's Vision"*, (1809). Luigi Sabatelli (Italian, 1772 – 1850). Artvee. Public Domain.

Page 221. *"Salvator Mundi"*, Alvise Vivarini (Italian, ca.1445-1505). Artvee. Public Domain.

Page 227. *"Christus mit dem Lieblingsjünger"*, Johannes, Halbfiguren am Tisch des letzten Abendmahles, über ihnen die Dreifaltigkeit, (1874). Eduard von Steinle (Austrian, 1810 – 1886). Artvee. Public Domain.

Page 229. *"Judas Returns the Money"*, (Judas rend l'argent). James Tissot, (1836-1902). Brooklyn Museum Collections - Wikimedia Commons. Public Domain.

Page 238. *"Christus als Salvator Mundi met cherubijnen"*, Schelte Adamsz. Bolswert, after Peter Paul Rubens, (1596 – 1659). Rijksmuseum. Public Domain.

Other Books by
Fr. Marin de Boylesve:

A Thought for
Each Day of the Year

ISBN: 978-9893319956

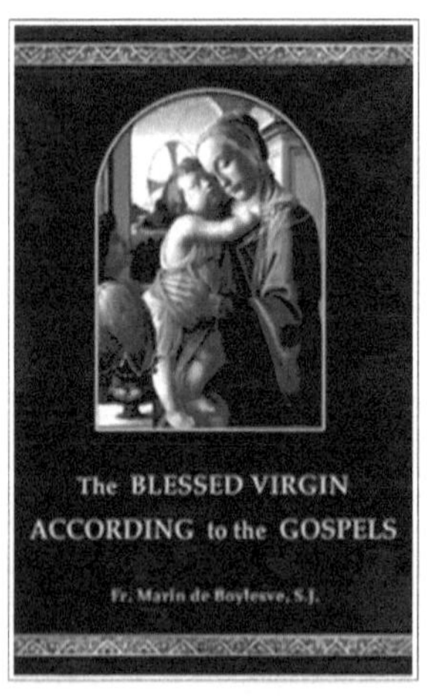

The Blessed Virgin
According to the Gospels

ISBN: 978-9895372607

**Little Month
of Saint Joseph**

ISBN: 978-9899684485

**The First
and Second Joseph**

ISBN: 978-989-53726-2-1

The Sacred Heart of Jesus

ISBN: 978-9893328071

The Month of the
Precious Blood

ISBN: 978-9893328088

The Month of
Saint Michael

ISBN: 978-9899684492

The Month of
Saint Teresa

ISBN: 978-9895372614

Month of Mary – Queen of France

ISBN: 978-989-53726-3-8

Devotion to Saint Ignatius

ISBN: 978-989-53726-4-5

Other books by E.A. Bucchianeri
by Subject

<u>Prophetic Visions:</u>

* We Are Warned: The Prophecies
of Marie-Julie Jahenny (E-book)

* Marie-Julie of the Crucifix:
Stigmatist and Prophet (E-book)

<u>The Faustian Legend:</u>

* Faust: My Soul be Damned for the World, 2 Vols.

<u>Lord of the Rings:</u>

* Lord of the Rings: Apocalyptic Prophecies
(E-Book)

Classical Music:

* Handel's Path to Covent Garden

* A Compendium of Essays:
Purcell, Hogarth and Handel, Beethoven, Liszt, Debussy
and Andrew Lloyd Webber

Fiction Novels:

* Brushstrokes of a Gadfly

* Vocation of a Gadfly

Phantom of the Opera:

* Phantom Phantasia: Poetry for the
Phantom of the Opera Phan

www.ingramcontent.com/pod-product-compliance
Lightning Source LLC
Chambersburg PA
CBHW021944120726
47992CB00001B/142